Burns and the Sugar Plantocracy of Ayrshire

Eric J Graham

Designed and
Published by
MDPD, Edinburgh
enquiries@mdpd.co.uk

Front cover:
'Cutting the Cane' from *Ten Views of Antigua* by William Clark

Back cover:
'The Betrothal of Robert Burns and Highland Mary' by James Archer

Eric Graham was educated at Kilwinning High School and Irvine Royal Academy Ayrshire. He is a graduate of Strathclyde and Exeter Universities where he studied Scottish and Maritime History respectively. His doctoral thesis provide the core of his first book *A Maritime History of Scotland (1650 – 1790)*. He has since been published widely in learned journals and is a regular reviewer. His other books include the acclaimed *Seawolves: Pirates and the Scots* (shortlisted for the Saltire Prize for Scottish History Book of the Year in 2006) and *Clyde Built: Blockade Runner, Cruisers and Armoured Rams of the American Civil War*. He has made a number of radio and television appearances as an expert historian.

Dr Graham is currently an honorary post doctoral fellow of the Scottish Centre for the Diaspora at Edinburgh University, Historical Advisor to the Historic Scotland's Trinity House Project and the Ulster Historical Foundation and Project Consultant to University College London's *Structure and Significance of British Caribbean Slave Ownership 1763-1833* project.

Further information is available on his website: www.ericgraham.co.uk.

Contents

Acknowledgements

I would very much like to express my gratitude to my friends Tom Barclay, Mark Duffill, Iain Whyte and Stephen Mullen for their invaluable contribution to this study. Tom has been a stalwart; piecing together the intricate genealogies of the Ayrshire families mentioned. Mark has been more than generous in sharing his extensive research on the Cunyngham family plantation records and court cases. Stephen and Iain's roles have been to keep me up to date on current research on Scotland's involvement in black slavery and its abolition.

My thanks also extends to the staff of Ayrshire Archives who, whilst moving premises, facilitated my searches under difficult circumstances. Also to the publications team of the Ayrshire Archaeological & Natural History Society who published the original version as a monograph in 2009. I would also like to acknowledge the *Legacies of British Slave Ownership* database compiled by University College London which has provided additional material for this revised edition.

The artist Graham Fagen very kindly gave permission to use his drawings of eighteen century shipping adverts. All other illustrations are, unless stated otherwise, provided by the author.

A special mention must also be made of the images provided by the Faillie family, Chile, and the open access granted by the present Fergusson family to the 'Fergusson of Kilkerran' papers and plantation maps which so enrich this study.

Finally, to my wife Jan who makes all things possible.

Eric J Graham
University of Edinburgh 2014

Foreword

It is well-known that but for the early success of the ' Kilmarnock edition' of his poetry Robert Burns, like so many young Scotsmen of his generation, would have taken ship in 1786 for employment in the sugar plantations of Jamaica. In this illuminating study, based entirely on research on contemporary documents, Eric Graham has pieced together the strange world which the Bard might have entered if good luck had not smiled on him.

Only now is the story of Scottish involvement in the Caribbean economy starting to be told in full detail. It is one of the darker episodes of the nation's history. Though the Scots were not much concerned in the direct transatlantic slave trading in which Bristol and Liverpool specialised, they were deeply involved in the plantation economies which could not have existed and flourished without a pitiless system of chattel black slavery. In Jamaica, for instance, Scots were preeminent as plantation owners, overseers, bookkeepers, soldiers and physicians. It was a society governed by greed, the lust for profit and the unrelenting exploitation of many thousands of hapless slave labourers. As one observer remarked: *the state of society in this place is as low and degraded as it is possible to conceive - a perfect Sodom!*

Dr Graham examines the involvement of some of Ayrshire's social elite in the Caribbean. He shows how it was commonplace for younger sons to seek their fortunes on the islands of the British Caribbean. If they survived the lethal tropical diseases, which gained for the West Indies the unenviable title of 'the white man's grave', the aim was to make money quickly and return home to Scotland with the profits - living out the rest of their lives as members of the landed gentry. So it was riches obtained from the slave plantations that fuelled estate purchases and financed agricultural improvement in eighteenth century Scotland.

The picture that Eric Graham draws could be replicated in many other parts of the country. But, by providing a detailed case study of Ayrshire's links to the eighteenth century transatlantic empire, he succeeds in adding important pieces of invaluable evidence to an aspect of our history that many generations of Scots preferred to forget.

Professor TM Devine OBE BA, PhD, DLitt, Hon DLitt (Strathclyde), Hon DLitt (Queen's, Belfast), Hon DLitt (Abertay), FRHistS, FSAScot, FRSE, Hon MRIA, FBA. Personal Senior Research Chair of History; Scottish History (Edinburgh).

Introduction

Will ye go to the Indies, my Mary,
And leave auld Scotia's shore?
Will ye go to the Indies, my Mary,
Across th' Atlantic roar?

In the early summer of 1786, Robert Burns, with his chest packed, awaited the summons to embark on the brig *Nancy* at Greenock dock for a new life in Jamaica with his love Margaret Campbell - 'Highland Mary'. As he lay in hiding from the warrant he believed the father of the pregnant Jean Armour had attained for his arrest, he penned the light-hearted poem *On a Scotch Bard Gone to the West Indies*. Of the ten verses, only the penultimate reflects his concern at his reception in the sugar islands:

Jamaica bodies, use him weel,
An' hap him in a cozie biel:[1]
Ye'll find him ay a dainty chiel,
An' fou o'glee:
He wad na wrang'd the very Diel,
Tho' owre the Sea!

The fugitive Burns, it would appear, was determined to quit Ayrshire and Scotland. In June he wrote from Kilmarnock, somewhat melodramatically, to his friend David Brice that his ship was set to leave imminently *to take me out to Jamaica, and then, farewel dear old Scotland, and farewel dear, ungrateful Jean, for never, never will I see you again.*[2] Burns, of course, did not get as far as the gang plank of the *Nancy*. The tragic death of 'Highland Mary' while waiting for him at Greenock and the success of his first 'Kilmarnock edition' of his *Poems, Chiefly in the Scottish Dialect* turned him towards the saloons and clubs of Edinburgh and on to national acclaim.

---

1   In modern terminology; 'a cosy billet'.

2   National Library of Scotland, Watson Collection MS 586.

For SAVANNAH-LA-MARR, JAMAICA,
to call at ANTIGUA,

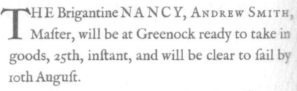

THE Brigantine NANCY, ANDREW SMITH, Mafter, will be at Greenock ready to take in goods, 25th, inftant, and will be clear to fail by 10th Auguft.

For freight or paffage, apply to James Brown, infurance-broker, Glafgow, or to the Mafter at Greenock.

Glafgow, 12th July, 1786.

Drawing of the Advert for the sailing of the *Nancy Glasgow Mercury* 6-15 July 1786

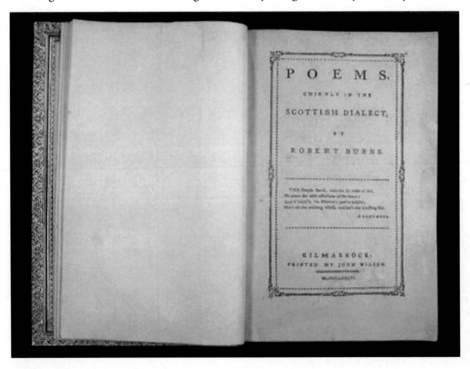

The Kilmarnock Edition

Studies of this fateful episode in his life invariably dwell on his motives and immediate personal circumstances, primarily: the repudiation and 'mutilation' of his 'marriage attestation' by Jean and the threat of legal action by her family. In addition, there was the dire economic prospect of the Mossgeil farm, the lease to which Burns signed over to his brother Gilbert in anticipation of his departure. A few authorities venture further and allocate a few lines of conjecture as to the moral dilemma that Burns – the author of - *a man's a man for a' that* - would have faced had he gone.[3] Understandably, the historical line of enquiry stops at the shoreline of Scotland.

The aim of this study is to straddle the Atlantic in order to gain an understanding of the *Jamaica bodies* - the 'sugar plantocrats' - whose estates were so conspicuous in the physical and social landscape of eighteenth century Ayrshire as well as in the West Indies.[4] Burns looked to this elite for an escape route, advancement and a *cozie biel* far removed from his troubles. In undertaking this review it is also hoped to reveal the extent of Burns' naive expectations and poor understanding of the lifestyle of a bookkeeper on a Jamaican plantation in the final quarter of the eighteenth century.

---

3   A notable exception is Gerard Carruthers 'Burns & Slavery', *Fickle Man,* (eds) Johnny Rodger & Gerard Carruthers, (Dingwall, 2009).

4   The archives deployed in this study are primarily those held by the National Archives of Scotland (NAS) and the Ayrshire Archives (AA) and private papers listed on the National Register of Archive of Scotland (NRAS). Collated, these provide some of the earliest and most complete records on British involvement in black chattel slavery to have survived. Spelling in italic indicates 'as found' (sic) or the best that can be deciphered from the original documents.

Chapter 1

Burns & Jamaica

As Burns was composing his farewell odes in June 1786, Charles Douglas wrote to his elder brother - Dr Patrick residing at Garrallan, Old Cumnock, Ayrshire - from their Ayr Mount plantation in Jamaica.[5] In his two page letter he reported that his new slave overseer, Peter Smith, and his bookkeeper, Cathcart Hutchison, were both doing *very well*. He also noted that since the end of the American War of Independence three years earlier, well paid higher positions in the sugar plantations had all but vanished: *Young doctors are very plenty here many of them much at a loss to get employment in that way.* The prospect of a 'good living' and advancement for a local Ayrshire lad of lesser skills and no capital had also all but vanished.

Garrallan House

5   Patrick Douglas had probably practised medicine in Jamaica and, like so many young Scottish surgeons, had acquired his plantations (usually through marriage) whilst there. He is, arguably, better known to history as a partner in the Ayr Bank (Douglas Herron & Co) which failed in 1772. He had succeeded to the Garrallan estate in 1776 and was later surgeon to the West Lowland Fencibles. His principal plantation holding was listed in the *Jamaica Almanack* of 1811 as the 'Ayr Mount' plantation (65 slaves and 28 livestock) upon which was the main residence called 'Spring bank' three miles inland from Port Antonio in the parish of Portland. His other holding was the Nightingale Grove – presumably an animal 'pen' - which most sugar plantations possessed: being highly depended on animal manure and draught animals. In 1811 the management of the holdings was entrusted to John Steele – the replacement for Charles. In 1835 James Steele (presumably a descendent or relation of John Steele) and his four sisters 'of Portland' claimed the compensation for the loss of their slaves.

Charles concluded his letter with a request for another bookkeeper. *The young fellow I want is one that can write & read as to be able to answer a letter I might write to him while I am abroad – a Poor boy or any other Lad I suppose you may get enough for 10 or 12 pounds a year of less.*[6] His brother had already recruited an unlikely new bookkeeper for him - the twenty-seven year old forlorn local farmer and aspiring poet Robert Burns.

Prior to his departure for Jamaica, Burns attended a soiree hosted by Dr Patrick, at which the surgeon's immediate neighbours - James Whyte of Glaisnock, Old Cumnock and his wife (described by Burns as 'Jamaicans') - were present.[7] He recalled that they advised him strongly to reconsider his choice of sailing *which derange my plans altogether*. The naïve Burns, no doubt anxious to leave Scotland to evade his pursuers, had intended to embark on the earliest available passage to Jamaica on the brig *Nancy*, Captain Andrew Smith, due to sail from Greenock on 10 August for the port of Savannah-La-Mer via Antigua. This final landing place, the Whytes pointed out, was in the extreme south west of the island. To reach Port Antonio (two hundred miles away by rough road) entailed skirting the 'cockpit country' inhabited by armed bands of 'maroons' and a tortuous circumnavigation of the spinal Blue Mountains.[8] Far better, they thought, that he should wait a month for the sailing from Greenock on the *Bell*, Captain John Cathcart, for the Windward Islands and Kingston, Jamaica. From Kingston to Port Antonio was a much more acceptable distance (sixty miles) and through much less hazardous terrain.

---

6   This letter is held by the Burns Monument Trust.

7   The Whytes must have only just returned from Port Antonio area as Charles
         Douglas refers to a 'James White' in his letter to his brother, commending him as an
         acquaintance who could readily explain the current state of his business dealings.
         It would seem likely that the Whytes would meet Burns again, as their farm in
         Dumfriesshire - Over Stroquhan - was close to Ellisland. Burns took up the lease for
         this farm in March 1788, shortly after his return from Edinburgh.

8   'Maroon' is Spanish for 'wild ones'. They were the descendants of escaped slaves, who
         had previously fought the British army to a standstill and who had extracted a treaty
         from the British in 1738. They were divided into two distinct camps – the Leeward
         and Windward groups. The most rebellious group was eventually rounded up by the
         military and deported in 1795 - firstly to Nova Scotia and finally to Sierra Leone.

It would seem fairly certain that his future employer and his Jamaican advisors were unaware of his intention to take Margaret Campbell with him. Thirty years earlier bringing out a supportive 'wife' might have been condoned. But by the 1780s a single profit-driven manager and overseer was the norm. Two years before Burns' intended departure, the Rev. James Ramsay of Fraserburgh (who had been driven out of St Kitts by planter hostility after twenty years service) wrote an essay deploring the replacement of the married manager by the *dissipated, careless, unfeeling young man, or a grovelling, lascivious old batchelor (each with his half score of black or mulattoe pilfering harlots).*[9] One Scots apothecary working on the Fraser Bowden estate in St. Thomas in the East wrote back to his sister in Greenock in 1787 stating that: *the West Indies is the last place in which I would wish any female friend of mine.*[10] Indeed, towards the end of the century it was exceedingly rare for a white woman to come out to a plantation other than as the wife or daughter of an established wealthy planter or senior official and even then was typically accompanied by a suitable entourage.

What life would have been like for the Bard and his consort had they stepped off the gangplank at Kingston can be surmised from commentaries left by other Scottish lads who arrived in Jamaica.[11] Surviving the initial exposure to the tropical climate and disease was the first hurdle for all newcomers. The young trainee bookkeeper - Alexander Moutiers of Edinburgh - wrote home soon after landing Kingston in the rainy season of 1729: *I shall give you a small notion of this place; the island is very pleasant to the eye, but the most unhealthy, and fatall to new comers ... people dying in such plenty they busy bury[ing] vast quantitys just now and they no more regard a fellow's dying here than if he were a negroe. I was not two days ashore when I had what they call a 'seasoning' which was a feaver continued with me for two days very violent, but bless God I escaped*

---

9   James Ramsay, *Essays on Slavery* (1784). Dubbed the 'Unknown Abolitionist', Ramsay was one of the key figures in the movement to end the slave trade.

10   John Clark to his sister Peggy in Greenock. Letter dated 23 July 1787, NLS Acc.7285.

11   For the background behind these two accounts see: Eric J Graham, 'Abolitionists and apologists: Scotland's Slave Trade Stories', *Discover NLS* Issue 6 (Winter 2007) pp. 20-22.

pretty well and should think myself lucky.[12] This 'seasoning' period was considered to last two years, after which life expectancy - for both white and black - improved somewhat. This largely explains why a bookkeeper's salary and the price of a slave were incrementally based on how long the individual had been on the island.

Then there was the cultural shock of entering into Jamaican society. The first view of Kingston for the boy apprentice Samuel Robinson of Wigtonshire was from the deck of his Liverpool slave ship – the *Lady Nelson* - in 1803. He was taken aback by the sight of *old gibbets with the iron framework in which the victims were suspended, swinging and shrieking on their rusty hinges, the sight of which made me shiver.* The thirteen year old sailor later recovered his nerve enough to enjoy the colour and sounds of this bustling port.

Mulatto woman with two black slaves

Samuel, even at his tender age, had no delusions as to what he had joined - a society perverted by slavery: *I do believe, from what has come under my observation while here, that the state of society in this place is as low and degraded as it is possible to conceive - a perfect Sodom! With the exception of those who have married in Europe, there is scarce such a thing heard of as marriage. Among the lower tribe prostitution is the order of the rule in every sense of the word. In the middle class concubinage is the order of the day.*[13]

---

12   Alexander Moutiers to Edward Burd 9 September 1792; NAS RH 15/54/9. Moutiers found a position as a bookkeeper to a Kingston apothecary who supplied drugs to Dr Aikenhead on the Hamilton plantations.

13   Samuel Robinson, *The Experiences of a Boy Sailor aboard a slave ship* (Hamilton, 1867), letter VIII, Jamaica, 1803, pp 119-154. He claimed his account was based on letters he had sent home as a boy.

He was, however, impressed by the unswerving loyalty of black and mulatto women *in their 'marriage' as they call it,* to their white partners.[14] The female children of their union invariably followed the same path into concubinage to escape labouring in the fields and so gained the social promotion that came with being 'lighter' skinned. He described the male off-spring as strolling around the town in high fashion dress and occasionally gathering at the quay side to jeer at the new 'salt water' African slaves being landed. Their common aim was to reach the classification of 'octoroon' (only one eighth African) at which point basic rights, such as taking a surname and owning property, were extended to them on most British islands.

Moutier, in his early twenties, was repelled by the hierarchy of 'pigmentocracy' ': *Our women they are generally Molattoes, as for my part I have such a detest to their colour that not once whetted my appetite (tho' they generally are worth a great deal of money). The negro girls are very plenty and it is cheaper injoying one of them than the our street walkers but to see the creatures walking up and down .... would turn the stomach of any modest young man like me, leatly come from a Christian country. As for those they call their white women, they seem to be God Almighty's unnacountables, they swear most untolerably, speak badly publicly and whore (not in the caution used in Britain) they drink very little – tea, coffee & chocolate being their chief drink, but as I am but a new commer amongst them I shall in my next letter be able to give you Gentlemen particular account of them.* In his later letters, Moutiers succumbs to the planters' way of life. He sends a black boy to Thomas Blackwood in Edinburgh to be apprenticed as a millwright; asks for a young lad with fair hair to be sent out as his bookkeeper on a four year indenture - *you might find such*

---

14   As Burns' platonic friend 'Clarinda' (Agnes 'Nancy' Maclehose) was also to find when she sailed on the well armed 'letter of marque' ship *Roselle* owned by William Sibbald & Co from Leith in February 1792, in order to attempt a reconciliation with her husband James then residing in Jamaica. When confronted he made it clear that he was happier living with his black mistress by whom he had a daughter. Nancy returned to Edinburgh after four months on the island. The *Roselle* was sunk with all hands by a Spanish warship on a subsequent passage.

a one in Harriiotes Hospital; and sets up house with a mulatto mistress whilst chasing the hand of a widow who he boasts is worth some money - *am maeking strong love to her [but] she still denys to hear my vows but I don't design to be put off.* [15]

This scenario was endemic throughout the sugar islands and had been from time immemorial. Janet Schaw of Lauriston, Edinburgh - the self styled 'Lady of Quality' who visited the Leeward islands in 1775 en route from Charleston - curtly put it down: *to Licentious and even unnatural amours of the white man ... which appear too plainly from the crowds of Mulattos, which you meet in the streets, house and indeed every where; a crime that seems to have gained sanction from custom ... the black wenches lay themselves out for white lovers, in which they are all to successful.*

An Edinburgh 'Lady of Quality'
by John Kay

She was greatly taken by the genteel manners of the few white women – the wives and daughters of planters – with whom she socialised. This is in direct contrast to the contempt in which he held the habits of their husbands: *Tho, they have fine women and such as might inspire any with sentiments that do honour to humanity yet they know no such nice distinctions ... I sincerely believe that they are excited to the crime by no*

---

other desire or motive but that of adding to the number of their slaves.[16]

In the Jamaican countryside, slave women on the plantations served the same function for the bookkeepers. Sundays was the white staff's day off and they congregated at one of the plantations for drinking sessions. The host was expected to have selected women for their pleasure.[17] Their mulatto offspring are to be found in most plantation slave lists, often as house servants or drivers.

The all pervasive cruelty that upheld the system is mentioned in another Scottish lad's account - that of Thomas Smith of Arbroath. He too had arrived at Kingston on a slaver from the Guinea coast in 1762. Revolted by what he had seen and done during the 'middle passage' he refused to re-engage for another slaving voyage and walked off his ship without taking his wages.

He soon found work on a coastal schooner trading between Port Antonio and Kingston. He recalled once walking the dusty land route between the two ports (as Burns and Mary would have had to do) in pitch black hearing nothing, as he perceived it, *but the roaring of wolves and Snakes.* He described the harbour of Port Antonio as having a large fortification with forty guns mounted, and at all times a party of soldiers. While ashore there he once witnessed the punishment of three runaway slaves – one a boy. They were *carried to the wharf, a place where they ship sugar, when both their hands were tied across the top of a beam, and thirty six pound weight fastened to each foot [to stretch the skin on their back] and whipped to such a degree, that the flesh was torn from sundry parts of their bodies. The number of stripes they received were thirty nine.*[18]

---

16   Janet Schaw, *Journal of a Lady of Quality*, edited by Evangeline Walker Andrews (Nebraska, 2005), pp. 112 & 154.

17   This creole life style in Jamaica in 1816 was graphically described in a novel about a young Scotsman *Marly; or, A Planter's Life in Jamaica* (anon) edited by Karina Williamson (Oxford, 2005).

18   Thomas Smith, *Narrative of an unfortunate voyage to the coast of Africa* (Arbroath, 1813), pp.62-3.

View of Port Antonio

How the great humanist Burns, or for that matter Margaret Campbell, would have coped with entering this degenerate and unjust society at the lowest social level for whites, will no doubt remain a matter for debate *ad infinitum*. In his defence, it must be emphasised that his plan had all the hallmarks of desperation. Financially, it was verging on lunacy. A one way passage to Jamaica cost around £9 sterling at the time. Whilst a small advance against wages was usually offered by the planter to those signing indentures, the cost of passage was invariably down to the new employee.[19] In the case of Burns, with 'Highland Mary' in tow, this would have doubled. Leaving little change from the £20 he had made from selling the rights to his poetic works. His first year's annual salary would have barely recouped this initial outlay.[20]

---

19   This was to ensure that the employer did not lose too much to servants who did not turn up to serve their indentured time - which was normally three years.

20   Wages for a bookkeeper at this time varied between £20-£40 sterling per annum depending on experience and was usually incremental over the indenture period.

Had he married her in transit or on arrival at Jamaica, he would also have thrown away his only realistic route for advancement in the islands - marrying a rich widow or her daughter. This had been the prime objective of all who had left Ayrshire before him. As the one time Lord Mayor of London, John Barnard, counselled all aspiring young men: *A fair Wife with empty pockets is like a noble house without furniture, Showy, but useless.*[21]

---

21   John Barnard, *A present to the Apprentice or a Sure Guide to Wealth and Esteem* (London, 1807) p.150.

Chapter 2

Jamaica Bodies - the Hamiltons, Fergussons & Hunter Blairs

From the 1640s onwards the Guild Brothers of the Royal Burgh of Ayr had redirected their entrepreneurial energies across the Atlantic. The push westwards was occasioned by internal civil strife and foreign war which had dislocated their old European trade routes. Ayr's location, on the north western seaboard, away from the main theatres of war, was ideal.

The advent of the highly proscriptive English Navigation Acts presented a block to their ambitions. Aiding and abetting their breach of these Acts were the English officers of the Cromwellian garrison at Ayr who had married daughters of leading Guild members. The early ventures were to the English islands of Barbados and St. Kitts.[22]

The upheaval of the 'Glorious Revolution' of 1688 and the commencement of the second 'Hundred Years War' with France offered a prime opportunity for young Ayrshire merchants to enter the plantation business in earnest. Three families are central to this study: the Hamiltons of Ayr, the Oswalds of Auchencruive and the Cunynghams of Glengarnock.

The Jamaican Bodies – The Hamiltons

The first of this dynamic family to go out to the West Indies was Hugh

---

22   See: Tom Barclay & Eric J Graham, *The Early Transatlantic Trade of Ayr (1640-1730),* Ayrshire Archaeological and Natural History Society [AANHS] monograph 30 (Ayr, 2005).

Hamilton of Clongall.[23]   He was born into Ayr's close knit merchant community. His father (Robert I) was the Baillie Clerk of Carrick while his mother (Janet) was daughter of the local merchant John Blackwood.[24] Hugh's first overseas venture came unstuck in August 1689 when he was captured, along with his cousin Andrew Cathcart, on their homeward passage from the islands by French privateers and subsequently held prisoner in St. Malo. Four months later their fathers petitioned the Scottish Privy Council to exchange them for two Catholic priests who had been arrested and imprisoned in Scotland.[25] As it transpired Andrew made good his own escape leaving only Hugh to be exchanged. Undeterred, Hugh was partner in another transatlantic voyage, that of the *Joseph & Daniel* to Virginia in 1693, which resulted in protracted litigation.[26]

Two years earlier Hugh had married Jean Ferguson, daughter of the lawyer John Ferguson of Castlehill. They had seven daughters and three sons. The latter are referred to hereafter as Robert II, John I and Hugh II. It was the two eldest sons who carved out a sugar empire in Jamaica. This was then consolidated by succeeding generations in the family, namely: John II, Hugh III and Alexander West (son of John II).[27] The wealth amassed from the produce of slavery (sugar, rum, molasses, coffee, cotton and indigo) financed the establishment of their respective family seats - Rozelle, Sundrum, and Pinmore & Belleisle - in the southern hinterland of Ayr.[28]

---

23   Clongall or Glengall is in Alloway.

24   Janet's brother - Robert Blackwood of Pitreavie - was a staunch supporter of the attempts to found 'Scots Lots' in the New World investing in the Carolina, the East New Jersey and the Darien schemes. See: Tom Barclay & Eric J Graham, 'The Covenanters Colony in Carolina', *History Scotland* (Vol.4, No.4, July 2004).

25   Hugh's uncle was listed as 'Heugh Cathcart of Cairletoune' [Girvan]. The two priests were Andrew Fairfoull held in Inverness and a 'Seatton' held in Blackness castle. *Register of the Privy Council of Scotland* (3rd series Vol. XIV, entry dated 19 December 1689).

26   Barclay & Graham, *The Early Transatlantic Trade of Ayr* pp. 45-8.

27   Hugh II stayed at home becoming a Minister of Religion in Girvan and died in 1788.

28   Robert II was born 5 January 1698, John on 24 March 1702 and Hugh on 6 January 1707.

Robert II

Robert, the eldest son of Hugh I, was the key to the family's future fortunes. The timing of his departure to Jamaica was almost certainly triggered by the

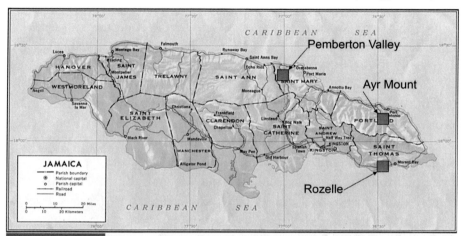

The Plantations   The South Ayrshire Jamaican Plantations

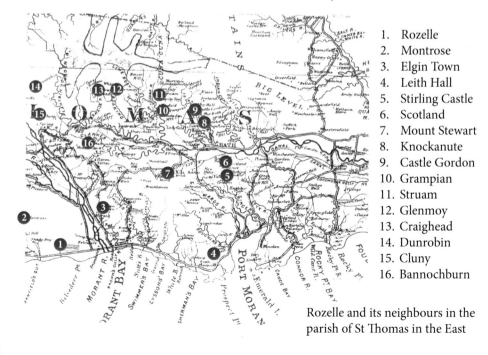

1. Rozelle
2. Montrose
3. Elgin Town
4. Leith Hall
5. Stirling Castle
6. Scotland
7. Mount Stewart
8. Knockanute
9. Castle Gordon
10. Grampian
11. Struam
12. Glenmoy
13. Craighead
14. Dunrobin
15. Cluny
16. Bannochburn

Rozelle and its neighbours in the parish of St Thomas in the East successful petition by the Guilds of the Royal Burgh of Ayr for the restoration of their port's right to trade directly in colonial goods (tobacco and sugar).[29] Once in Jamaica he did not lose much time establishing himself. Within a year of his arrival, in July 1734, he had married Jean Mitchell, the widow of a successful planter.[30] She was one of the island's established plantocracy whose 'seasoned' womenfolk followed the tradition of 'marry them and bury them' as the means to preserve their possessions and maintain their social status. Robert was her third husband.

On their wedding he was instantly elevated to the planter class. She brought two large working plantations - 'Pemberton Valley' in the parish of St Mary and 'Rozelle' in the parish of St. Thomas in the East - plus £3,000 sterling to the union.[31] There were, however, complications. While Jean held the Pemberton Valley plantation in her own right (she had inherited it from her father, 'Old' Thomas, on his death in 10 June 1720), her claim to her father's Rozelle plantation was hotly contested by Dorothy, the widow of her brother 'Young' Thomas, who had died in January 1733.[32]

When Robert first arrived on the scene, Jean and her second husband, Major James Garth, were locked in a battle over Dorothy's claim on one third of the Rozelle slaves. Three months later, matters were greatly complicated with the death of Garth (October 1734) who was then thirty seven years old.[33]

---

29   Robert sent two hogsheads of island tobacco back to Ayr on the *Brothers* of Ayr, Captain John Orr, and a further 131 hogsheads on the *Prosperity* of Ayr, Captain Alexander Creighton, late 1734 or early 1735.

30   In some legal documents she is referred to as 'Jane'. Old Thomas died in 10 June 1720.

31   She also inherited a moiety (half) of the small Stanton plantation close by Rozelle which may have been sold before her wedding to Robert as it does not appear in the later business accounts. The legalities of the ownership of the Rozelle estate was further complicated by its physical composition – being made up of different land parcels, the core of which was those once belonging to Clement Richardson. The estate layout was not well consolidated as it was almost dissected by the lands of the neighbour - Mr James Watt.

32   It would appear that Jean had the legal right to Rozelle by her father's will but her brother had occupied the estate as a tenant on the death of his father.

33   He had been a major in Lord Shannon's Troop of Horse Guards.

In such a litigious and male dominated society, a combatant husband was an essential element in the defence of an inheritance. So it is, perhaps, understandable that Jean's period of mourning prior to marrying Robert the following September was, even by Jamaican standards, a short one.[34]

With her new husband she succeeded in attaining Letters of Administration over the estates of her father, ending the claims on the lands of Rozelle. This was not, however, an end to the matter as the Stout family (Dorothy had since remarried) laid a fresh claim for a third of Rozelle's annual profits as her 'dowager portion'.[35]

Adding to the Hamiltons' problems was yet another new lawsuit. This one was filed by the Miller family (Jean's first husband) for a share of the Pemberton Valley estate.[36] Such opportunistic litigation was then commonplace on the sugar islands, where the courts were susceptible to pressure from local vested interests. Indeed, those following a change of ownership were often successful when the new owner was absent from the island. Robert was, however, in situ and vigorously fought both causes through the Kingston courts, winning both after conceding a reduced dowager portion to Dorothy in her lifetime.[37]

In the meantime, he extended his new empire to include management of the Borndon plantation in which 'Young' Thomas and a close associate - Basnett - held an interest. Help was also to hand when Robert's younger

---

34   Robert took immediate control of the slaves who were then complaining about their condition and some had run away. Robert blamed this on the slack behaviour of the overseer and handed out severe punishments to restore his authority: AA DC 17/1.

35   Dorothy's maiden name was 'Slaughter'.

36   Jean first married Pauncefoot (or Pauncefort) Miller - the overseer of the Pemberton Valley estate - by whom she had a child. Tragically the boy died aged only six. Pauncefoot died not long afterwards, aged 45, in January 1728. He left her the bulk of his possessions and £5,000 sterling. George Miller, brother of Pauncefort, was the main pursuant in this claim. The counterclaim was that Pauncefort had huge debts to his father-in-law.

37   When the Rozelle plantation was sold in 1764 this obligement was passed on. By then she was married to her sixth husband – a Captain Reyton of the 74th Foot.

brother John, having resigned from the Royal Navy, joined him in Jamaica as co-owner of the Pemberton Valley estate.[38] Unfortunately, John was lost at sea when returning home to see his new born son late in 1739.[39]

With the legal disputes over his ownership of his estates apparently settled in his favour and the revenue flow seemingly secure, Robert (now in his mid 40s), felt confident enough to realise his ambition to leave control of his plantation in the hands of his managers and return to Ayrshire. This had always been his intention, as he confided in a letter to Thomas Garvine back in Ayr in August 1740. *I am now resolv'd in all Events … to leave this island, in two or three years at the most, by which tyme I am in great hopes, I shall my matters brought to an issue, without which …there can be no retiring with true satisfaction.* In the same letter he stated *my ambition never aim'd higher, than that of being Independent [of means], and having it in my power to be usefull & serviceable to my friends, I am hopefull I shall be able to find my Self in these circumstances when my scatter'd affairs are brought*

John Hamilton - Brother of Robert

---

38   John and Robert invested in the transatlantic slave trade by buying a stake in cargoes ahead of delivery: *N.B: the condition of my brother and my standing this part [one eighth] of the ship and cargo is expressly on her cargoe of slaves being consigned to us.* AA DC 17/113. This extract and others on the Hamilton involvement can be viewed on the Ayrshire Archives 'Black History Month' website: http://www.ayrshirearchives.org.uk/exhibition/blackhist/index.htm.

39   The young John had married Margaret Montgomerie in 1730. She was the daughter of Hugh Montgomerie, the grandson of Alexander 6th Earl of Eglinton. Her brother Alexander's son Hugh, husband of Eleanora Hamilton would eventually succeed as the 12th Earl in 1796.

together.[40] This sentiment was shared by many Scottish planters anxious to repatriate their wealth from their investment in land and slaves in Jamaica. This was invariably a lengthy process as the collection of outstanding debts was notoriously difficult once back in Scotland.

His timing was finally dictated by Jean's failing health. They arrived back at Portsmouth in June 1744 with their four daughters – Jean, Frances, Margaret and Eleanora. Travelling north, they took up residence in Bourtreehill House, near Irvine which he leased. Within a year, however, his wife was dead.

Bourtreehill House

From his Ayrshire estate, Robert (assisted by an unmarried sister in the upbringing of his daughters) managed his affairs in Jamaica (including his widowed sister-in-law's share) via a stream of correspondence carried by the packets that regularly sailed between Greenock and Jamaica. The day-to-day running of his plantations had been left to a trusted overseer - James Stirling.[41] The overview of the estates' development, however, lay with his long standing business partner - Patrick Adams - who had been granted Powers of Attorney as factor by Robert on his departure. This arrangement

---

40   Robert Hamilton to Thomas Garvine 31 August 1740. AA DC 17/113. Dr Garvine led an extraordinary life: he worked in Peter the Great's hospital in St Petersburg and travelled across Siberia to the Chinese Imperial court before returning to Ayr where he served several spells as Provost.

41   Whilst it cannot be said with absolute certainly who he was, it is highly likely that he was the young fortune seeker James Stirling of Keir who had arrived in Jamaica with his brother around the same time as Robert.

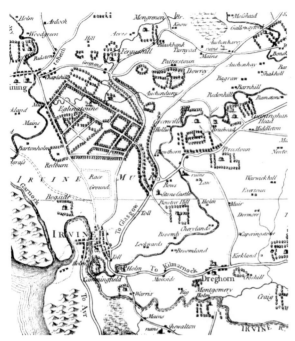

Detail of Armstrong's 1775 map of Ayrshire showing Bourtreehill, Broomlands, Eglinton and Ashenyards Estates.

was the accepted practice of the day.[42]

At first things did not go smoothly in his absence. One setback was an Act of God. On 20 October 1744 a great hurricane slammed into Jamaica flattening the cane, killing livestock and 'spooking' some of his slaves into running away.[43] Other setbacks were man-made. The 'go-ahead' Stirling found Adams' lack of support for his management galling. *We have four Negroes in the plantation which never stay at home. I wish you would be so good as to order Mr. Adam to ship them off for they are of no manner of service here and only a charge on your plantation.*[44]

The other advisor blocking Stirling's ambitious plans for the Pemberton Valley estate was Dr. William Aikenhead.[45] Aitkenhead rejected Stirling's plan to maximise the crop yield by buying or hiring additional slaves.

---

42   Charles Douglas complained in his letter to his brother Patrick that he had lost the opportunity to make £2000 sterling because the owner of a neighbouring estate – a Mr Ballantine – had not given him Power of Attorney to manage his workforce: *I dare not carry out the negroes to work.*

43   A month after the hurricane two women and a boy were still missing. James Stirling later followed the same matrimonial pathway to success and fortune. James Stirling to Robert Hamilton 20 October 1745, AA DC 17/113.

44   Ibid, 17 July 1745.

45   Alexander Moutier was his supplier of drugs – including mercurial ointments.

According to Stirling they were needed to extend the area that could be manured prior to planting more sugar canes. The doctor also blocked his scheme to clear more land for a large new pasturage which would allow an increase in the cattle herd (for manure and to provide the animal power for a new cane crushing mill).[46]

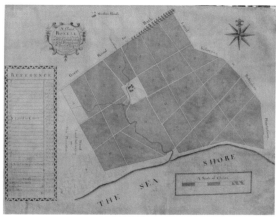

Rozelle plantation composition by previous owners (left). Rozelle plantation cane fields survey (right).

Robert's retirement was also upset by the mayhem of the Jacobite Rebellion at home and yet another claim by relatives of the dowager Dorothy on the profits of the Rozelle plantation.[47] The first problem was resolved on Culloden Moor in 1746, which encouraged Robert to buy the Bourtreehill estate. The second issue was adeptly handled by Patrick Adams and Dr Aikenhead through the Kingston Courts. The case was dismissed with costs granted against the pursuer the following year.[48]

---

46   He wanted to clear 100 acres for this purpose.

47   Stirling (from a staunch Jacobite family) commiserated with Robert on having to live though the upheaval: *I wish you were here yourself and out of our poore distrest country which I am now told is prodigiously pillaged by the Chevalier's Army. God send you Peace and Protect You & Yours from all Dangers.* AA DC 17/113.

48   For a while the claimant Abraham Richardson of Normandy and Jamaica (who Adams describes as *a pretended relative of Dorothy*) was paid off but this was soon stopped. Thomas Straton ended his 1749 yearly account of Rozelle expenditure for that year: *allowing nothing to Mr Richardson in right of the Brown dower.* AA DC 17/110.

This was the last legal challenge to the family's Jamaican assets.

Less successful were the attempts to raise production and hence profits from his prime Jamaican property. His frustrated overseer - the forward thinking James Stirling - had left to run his own plantation in the St James parish, having married well. His replacement - Peter Barclay - does not appear to have been of the same calibre. In October 1747 Robert wrote to Dr. Aikenhead: *Pemberton Valley often dissappoints us, and I must say it is one Estate that has hither to be most ungrateful considering what has been laid out upon it, however I am hopefull it will now begin to raise business, tho, by the by, it is what I cannot persuade my Sister in Law to believe, for which indeed I cannot much blame her, as she has been so often disappointed in the expectations she had had reason to entertain of it.*[49]

The Rozelle Mansion, Alloway

Rozelle House, Alloway

---

49   Robert Hamilton to Dr William Aikenhead: AA DC 17/113.

Detail of Armstrong's 1775 Map of Ayrshire showing Rozelle, Belleisle, Sundrum and Auchencruive estates.

The turn of the new decade, however, heralded a period of stability in Scotland. With the price of sugar and rum climbing Robert moved up the Ayrshire social ladder. In 1753 he purchased 676 acres (including four farms) of the 2,300 acres on offer at the great public roup of the lands of the Barony of Alloway.[50] Underwritten by his Jamaican assets, Robert carved out a new estate with mansion house, (finished 1760) which he appropriately named 'Rozelle'.

In March of that year he remarried. His new wife was the well connected widow Anne Cunninghame.[51] His social standing was further sealed by the advantageous marriages of three of his daughters. The first was that of his eldest daughter Jean (born in Jamaica c.1735) to George Lindsay - the 21st Earl of Crawford – on Boxing Bay 1755, after a highly unusual prenuptial incident that raised eyebrows at the time.[52] Her father put

---

50   Trustees for estate of the son of deceased brother John I bought up the other lots – Carcluie, Barrhill and Blackhill – which brought the total acres purchased by the Hamiltons to just under half that on offer. See: Thomas Limon, 'The Roup of the Lands of Alloway', *Ayrshire in the Time of Burns*, AANHS (1959).

51   She was the daughter of William Cunningham of Brownhill, a prominent Ayr merchant and married John Hunter of Mainholm (died 1755). On her marriage to Robert (1760) her two sons by John – Lt. Colonel William Hunter of Mainholm and Brownhill (part owner of the Rozelle plantation) and James Hunter of Robertland (a banker and partner in Hamilton's plantations) - became Robert's stepsons.

52   Problems with her dowry settlement caused the engagement to be cancelled. Whereupon Jean disappeared from Bourtreehill only to emerge in Edinburgh where she tracked down and confronted her suitor. She then persuaded him to marry her without the dowry being agreed. Colonel Hunter referred to it as an *accidental marriage*.

aside his displeasure at her actions when, in May 1757, a devastating fire destroyed their first home in Kilbirnie Place Castle. To accommodate them he moved to his nearly completion Rozelle mansion so that that they might have his residence at Bourtreehill house. It is worth noting that Robert's gardener – William Urquhart – stayed on at Bourtreehill and was very friendly with the Bard's father, with whom he exchanged books.[53] It would seem more than likely that the Hamilton's Jamaican connections would have been mentioned at some time in their conversations.

'Sundrum John'

Business affairs in Jamaica, however, took a turn for the worse soon after the Alloway land sale. The output of sugar from the Pemberton valley plantation lurched into serious declined. The blame was laid at the door of the new manager, the novice Thomas Straton, who had allowed himself to be *villainously imposed on by a worthless old fellow*.[54] Robert's solution was to send out his nephew John II, son of his drowned brother, as manager.

Born in 1739, John was in still in his teens when he arrived in Jamaica in early 1755. No doubt well prepared by his uncle, he set about a survey of the state of the estate.[55] Acting on his findings John, assisted by another new overseer – Thomas Paton – quickly rectified the neglect of the buildings, especially the worn out coppers in the all important boiler house, and pushed forward with the planting of rattans (cane saplings) to ensure a good crop the following year.

As part of his survey he took inventory of the prime assets on the estate (slaves and livestock). Of the former he found: 60 men (of whom 12 were 'distempered' and unfit for work) 40 women (of whom 7 were described as 'entirely useless'), 11 boys, 7 girls and 29 infants – making 147 souls in all. Of the livestock he listed; 48 cattle and 28 mules, each with a given

---

53   Mentioned in the 'Letters of Gilbert Burns'.

54   Probably the overseer Peter Barclay.

55   Letter from John Hamilton to Robert Hamilton, 27 January 1756: AA DC 17/113.

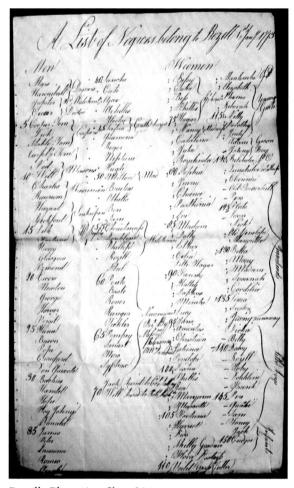

Rozelle Plantation Slave List

name similar in style to that given to the slaves.[56]

The much chastened manager Straton was given a second chance and moved to the Rozelle plantation. To ensure his success another new overseer, Ebenezer Campbell, was also appointed. Their joint management of the plantation was formalised with joint Powers of Attorney issue by Robert in late 1759. With this new management team in place John, then residing at Pemberton Valley, made plans to return to Ayrshire, unaware that dramatic events were to about to overtake him on the island.

The Perils of Plantation Life: Insurrection

Slave insurrections were the most feared aspect of life in the plantations where the ratio of black to white in the countryside was 50:1. While there

---

56   While the women and girls were given appropriate female names - Hannah, Nancy - many of the men and boys were often called after places - Scotland, Ayr, Hamilton, Pemberton and Galloway. Two males were noted as 'mulatto', i.e. of mixed race.

was a full garrison on the island and the militia was well armed, there was little chance of an uprising of slaves succeeding. But in 1760, at the height of the Seven Years War, the island's complement of regular soldiers had been stripped to strengthen the forces assaulting the neighbouring French islands. In British military history books 1760 is remembered as an 'annus mirabilis' when the Caribbean was virtually transformed into a British lake. In Black Caribbean History is it commemorated as the year of the first great blow in the fight against slavery.[57]

A Rebel Negra armed on his guard.

A Rebel Slave

This strike for freedom was hatched just eight miles away from Pemberton Valley by the legendary 'Tacky'- a slave on the Stirling's 'Frontier Estate' near Port Maria. He was in collusion with others on the neighbouring Trinity Estate owned by Zachary Bailey. Early in the morning of 7 April 1760 they rose as one and murdered their overseers. They then marched on Port Maria where they forced their way into the arsenal of the unguarded Fort Haldane taking forty muskets and four kegs of gunpowder. Now well armed, they descended onto the nearby Heywood Hall and Esher Estates inciting many of the slaves to join them. Thomas Straton reckoned they then numbered 110 in all and had

---

57   The 'Tacky Insurrection' is also called the 'Coromantine War' as the core fighters were slaves taken from the Coromantine Coast of Africa (modern day Ghana) into slavery. This area and the neighbouring Gold Coast were the prime source of slaves for the Jamaican market prior to 1776. Legend has it that Tacky was an Akan Chieftain taken as prisoner of war and sold into slavery. There is very little known about him or this landmark insurrection, other than that recorded by the contemporary commentator Edward Long in his *The History of Jamaica* (1774). This gives John Hamilton and his manager Thomas Straton's eye-witness accounts significance beyond that of local Scottish history.

already *Butchered & Killed some twelve white people and some Negroes.*[58]

In an attempt to contain the rebellion to the eastern half of the island, the few regular troops and dragoons which were available were rushed from Kingston to a form a 'cordon sanitaire' across the island. The local militia (all white males over fourteen years of age were obliged to serve) was then turned out to hunt them down. Writing to Robert from Kingston two weeks later, Straton the overseer, fretted for the safety of John trapped at Pemberton Valley. He took some relief from the knowledge that none of their estate slaves had joined the uprising. He was also pleased to conclude with the latest intelligence that most of the rebels had already been killed and that the remainder would be *hunted down quickly and will suffer that Shocking Punishment which their Crimes deserves.*[59]

His prediction was premature as 'Tacky' and his core band of the Coromantine rebels slipped through the cordon to reignite insurgence in the western parishes the following month. This rebellion was larger and more organised than the first outbreak and the future of white supremacy over black in Jamaica was in the balance. John Hamilton thought that 1,200 slaves were now 'out' and armed with weapons stolen from the houses they looted and burned. Containing them stretched the local militia to breaking point. Such was the perceived danger that the black maroons in the Cockpit Country were called upon to help - as per their treaty obligation. Marines from the few small naval ships that happened to be on station and sailors from merchant ships in the nearby ports were also landed. This unlikely combined force stormed the entrenched positions the rebels had thrown up near Green Island.

---

58   Thomas Straton to Robert Hamilton, AA DC 17/113. The Esher Estate was owned by William Beckford whose son married into the Hamiltons of Brodick.

59   The nature of these punishments can be surmised from the eye-witness account of Dr Walter Tullideph, a Scottish surgeon on Antigua during the suppression of a conspiracy amongst the slaves in 1736. *We are in a great deal of trouble in this island, the burning of negroes, hanging them on gibbets alive, racking them upon the wheel etc., takes up all our time.* Letter to his brother in St. Andrew, 15 January 1737, NAS GD 205/53/6.

It was a near run thing and the retribution was terrible and immediate. As Straton recorded with satisfaction; *they killed them with great slaughter and the prisoners they took, they hanged up without Ceremony or Judge or Jury.* 'Tacky' himself was shot dead by a maroon sharpshooter and his head mounted on a spike in Spanish Town. The mopping up was gruelling. John Hamilton, serving in the militia chasing the ones that got away, wrote home: *in great fatigue going into the woods after the Negro[e]s, obliged to put the [white] women and children onboard ships in the harbour. They murdered every white soul they laid hands on and in a cruell manner, there are still 100 out – it will hurt the island.*

The captured rebels were executed and mutilated, as Straton put it: *to leave a Terror in the minds of all the other Negroes in the future.* He noted that one of those executed was: *an old fellow and runaway from Pemberton Valley [who] was taken I believe on suspicion, condemned and executed and his head sent to [be] put on the mill.* Months later the last of the rebels 'at large' committed mass suicide rather than face a similar fate. All in all, it was not until October 1761 that the island's Governor could declare the emergency over.

After the bloodlust had run its course, measures were taken at Pemberton Valley to remove a major source of grievance with the male slaves. Straton (with John's approval) took the initiative: *I have lately purchased for the estate 6 Gold Coast Negro women which cost me £48 each ... which they are in great want off as the Negro men complained heavily.* This was, but one small act, that marked the easing of tension across Jamaica.[60]

With Straton stepping up to the mark, John finally retired back to Ayrshire. He brought back black servants with him: *In the village of Joppa on the main road from Ayr to Cumnock there were at one time a number of Negroes brought from the plantations in West Indies, belonging to John*

---

60   Thomas Straton to Robert Hamilton dated 16 February 1760 (by new calendar 1761)
        AA DC 13/133. This need for planters to take more care of their "property" eventually
        led to the Amelioration Acts passed by the local assemblies across the British islands
        in the 1820s. This was a rearguard action to counter mounting public indignation
        unleashed by the anti-slavery movement.

Sundrum John I by unknown artist   Sundrum John II by John Hoppner

Hamilton of Sundrum.[61] In 1762 and now in his majority, he married his cousin Lilias Montgomerie. The couple moved into the old Sundrum estate that his trustees had acquired for him prior to his departure to Jamaica.[62] The principal dwelling was an old established castle that they set about extending to accommodate their rapidly increasingly family. Even with his father's half share of Pemberton Valley, 'Sundrum John' (as he is referred to) was *pinched* for funds and sounded out the possibility of returning to Jamaica as manager of the family's Rozelle plantation. This was not to be.

---

61   *They intermarried with the local inhabitants, and traces of negro in hair and countenance could be observed for some generations;* unreferenced, as quoted by James Edward Shaw, *Ayrshire 1745 – 1970, A Social and Industrial History* (Edinburgh, 1953), p. 23. One such descendant was the master stone mason on the Sundrum estate, Alexander Waters, described as a Jamaican *man of colour* whose father was still alive in Jamaica at the time of his death. Obituary *Ayr Advertiser* 6 September 1894 as quoted by Rob Close, *Ayrshire Notes*, AANHS (Autumn, 2003) pp. 17-18.

62   The previous owner was James Murray of Broughton who sold his Auchencruive estate to the Oswalds a couple of years later. He invested heavily in the Ayr Bank and suffered severe losses.

The New Owners of the Rozelle Plantation

In June 1763 Robert was approached by Charles Montgomery of Broomlands (neighbour to his Bourtreehill estate) who had returned from Jamaica the previous year. Montgomery expressed a wish to buy the Rozelle plantation.[63] By December a deal was struck whereby Montgomery paid Robert £6,000 sterling for Rozelle, complete with slaves and livestock (£1,000 cash down payment and £5000 payable in four years with interest).[64] Montgomery soon reduced this liability by selling on a half share to Robert's step son Colonel William Hunter of Mainholm and Brownhill. Montgomery died in 1769 having paid Robert Hamilton in full. In his will he left his share of Rozelle to the banker Charles Fergusson, younger brother of Sir Adam Fergusson of Kilkerran. Matters did not rest there. The young Fergusson got into severe financial difficulties three years later when his bank - Charles Ferguson & Company of London – stopped payments on 10 June 1772. This precipitated the eventual collapse of the Douglas, Heron & Company (Ayr Bank) a year later.[65] Some time around 1782 Charles signed over his interest in Rozelle to this elder brother Sir Adam in lieu of the large cash advances he had received to save him from bankruptcy. Sir Adam was referred to by Burns as the 'Thee, 'aith -detesting chaste Kilkerran' in *The Author's Earnest Cry and Prayer.*[66]

---

63   Charles was the only son of Hugh Montgomery of Broomlands.

64   Copy of sundry letters, 20 December 1763. Montgomery was described as 'late merchant in Kingston': NRAS 3572/3/4, The Rozelle plantation was surveyed in 1772 as part of the transfer and described as 1650 acres of which 210 acres was then planted with cane, 7 acres pasturage and 1 acre of gardens: Ibid, 3572/38/2.

65   Charles' bank had been deeply involved with the first bank to default – Neale, James, Fordyce and Down of London – whose principal partner was his brother-in-law – Alexander Fordyce. The unscrupulous Fordyce was later blamed for triggering the crisis and fled to France. See: Frank Brady 'So Fast To Ruin'. *AANHS* Vol. 11, No.2, pp 25-44. Charles survived as a businessman and was the father of the 4th baronet.

66   NRAS, 3572/2/3. Sir Adam (1733-1813) was the 3rd baronet and an advocate. He was a shareholder of the failed Ayr Bank and strived to the last to save it. He was later elected MP for Ayrshire (three times) and Rector of Glasgow University beating Adam Smith for the Chair.

Sir Adam Fergusson by Henry Raeburn

In this convoluted way the Fergussons and the Hunter Blairs[67] came by the Rozelle plantation which they were to jointly own for the next seventy years. During this time they were absentee landlords administering their possession via a string of overseers of various abilities and trustworthiness - the first being John Paterson

The Montgomerie Connection

Financially secured by the proceeds of the sale of the Rozelle plantation, Robert Hamilton's status in Ayrshire society took a further boost in the summer of 1772.[68] As Colonel Hunter recalled, there was a family gathering at Rozelle House in Alloway attended by the Earl of Eglinton where a *certain affair [was] talked of* involving *Ellie and Montgomerie* that he thought would lead to a *matrimonial intention disclosure next week*. The *affair* was the marriage of Robert's youngest daughter – Eleanora – to Hugh Montgomerie of Coilsfield.[69]   This union further entwined the Hamilton and Montgomerie families.

---

67   James Hunter married the heiress Susan Blair of Dunskey, Wigtonshire, in 1770. In 1773 he changed the family name to Hunter Blair. Created baronet in 1786, he died the following year. His son David later inherited the Rozelle half share.

68   Charles Montgomery reckoned that Robert was already worth £30,000 before the sale and had settled £5,000 on his son-in-law John Ferguson of Greenvale.

69   Hugh Montgomerie was a military man whose career culminated with his appointment as Lt. Governor of Edinburgh Castle. He inherited the extensive Skelmorlie estate in North Ayrshire when his mother died in 1783. He was also the employer of the servant girl 'Highland Mary' when Burns first met her, and is said to have had an ongoing affair with her.

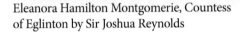

Eleanora Hamilton Montgomerie, Countess
of Eglinton by Sir Joshua Reynolds

'Sodger' Hugh Montgomerie 12th Earl
of Eglinton by John Singleton Copley

Robert Hamilton died that year. With no male heir, his eldest daughter Jean, the Countess Crawford, inherited his Ayrshire estates and his half share in the Pemberton Valley plantation in Jamaica. His will explicitly excluded her estranged and erring husband George from all aspects of the inheritance.[70] The Countess was very diligent in the management of her affairs, hosting the annual meeting of the other shareholders (Pemberton Valley and Rozelle were managed under a common umbrella after 1792) at Rozelle House until her death in 1809 aged seventy-three.[71]

---

70   They had five children before they separated over George's affair with another woman – Euphan Gourlay – by whom he also had children. The Crawfords eventually divorced.

71   Robert's widow Anne seems to have held a dowager portion as she attended the meeting of the trustees of the estates in 1789. She resided at Bourtreehill House for most of her later life. Robert's other three daughters shared a £800 legacy.

Hugh III

On Robert's death, the mantle of directly managing the Hamilton family's Pemberton Valley plantation passed to his nephew Hugh III - the son of Robert's youngest brother who had joined the ministry. Hugh was born in 1746, two years after his uncle's return to Ayrshire. As a young man he appears to have been taken to Jamaica by 'Uncle Robert' as part of his training for his future role as a plantation manager. This would have been in the late 1760s but the length of time they spent there is not known. What is certain is that Hugh was on the Pemberton Valley estate as factor, with the full support of his cousins, in 1776. [72]

His job was greatly facilitated by the business network that Uncle Robert and the other trustees had set up. The Ayr banker John Ballantine oversaw the payments to the shareholders and clearance of bills against the estates. [73] His brother Peter in Kingston acted in legal disputes in Jamaica. Somerville & Gordon of Greenock handled the shipping to the Clyde. [74] William Sibbald & Company did the same service at Leith. Herries & Company (connected to Robert's other step son - the banker James Hunter of Robertland) handled the shipments to and from London.

The American War of Independence

Much changed in the following decade, largely as a result of the American War of Independence (1776-83). This great upheaval blew a hole in the

---

72 Colonel Hunter Blair died in 1792 unmarried and without issue, leaving his estates to his nephew David who died soon afterwards. The half share of the plantation then passed to his brother James' son David. Thereafter, Hugh also held a watching brief over the Rozelle estate as one of the trustees of David while in his minority. The others were Sir Adam Fergusson of Kilkerran and the Countess Crawford.

73 John Ballantine looms large in Ayr's civil history. A celebrated Provost, he was a founder of Ayr Academy and planner of the new bridge over the river which Burns predicted would collapse.

74 The principal partners were William Somerville of Renfrew and James Gordon of Glasgow. This firm, under different names (Stirling & Gordon) became the largest West Indian trading house in Greenock.

British mercantilist system and dramatically altered security in the North Atlantic.[75] Losses to privateers at sea soon pushed up marine insurance rates to and from the Caribbean.[76] The rebellion of the American colonies also hit deliveries of foodstuffs to feed the slaves placing a premium on barrelled Scottish herring imported into Jamaica.

On the other hand, convoy delays and captures, drove up the price of sugar and rum in Europe making the risk more worthwhile.[77] The solution for the Hamiltons and their business partners – the Fergussons and Hunter Blairs - was to enter into a contract with the great Glasgow trading house of Alexander Houstoun & Company who ran a fleet of armed West Indiamen from the Clyde and also held interests in the 'sugarries' (refineries) in Greenock, Glasgow and Leith.[78]

In 1780 Hugh, while at Pemberton Valley, fell ill alarming his business partners: *We are all dispirited at you being so long missing and poor illness.*[79] He recovered but his health was a matter of ongoing concern. In the spring of 1781, as the war turned against Britain with the entry of the Dutch into the conflict, Sir Adam Fergusson considered selling off his half share of Rozelle. Losses at sea in the Caribbean soared, as Countess Crawford noted: *we are in great fears that the ship that was bringing our sugars is taken then was sixty six hogsheads sixty insured & the other six*

75   See: Eric J Graham, *A Maritime History of Scotland 1765-1790* (East Linton, 2002) pp. 249-290.

76   See: T M Devine, 'Transport Problems of Glasgow West India merchants during the American War of Independence, 1775-83' *Transport History* (1971) Vol. IV, pp.266-304.

77   At least one shipment of underinsured Hamilton sugar was captured. Another, onboard the *Isabella*, Captain McLenan, arrived safely in at Port Glasgow *having been long retarded.* Alexander Montgomery to James Hunter, 9 May 1779, AA DC 191/ bundle 45.

78   This was the greatest West Indies trading house in Scotland. It was founded by the McDowalls of Castlesemple, the Millikens of Milliken Park, the Houstouns of Jordanhill and the Raes of Old Govan. Their vessels were also privateers carrying 'letters of marque'.

79   John Ballantyne in Ayr to Hugh Hamilton in Jamaica, 31/12/1780 NAS GD 142/2/3.

& a puncheon of Rum not Insured.[80] At one stage, in early 1782, it looked likely that the French would attempt an invasion of Jamaica. In the crisis all able bodied white males were called to arms; as Hugh wrote *we are all soldiers* here.[81]

Tobago – *the 'Unfortunate Adventure'*

The biggest casualty of the war to the South Ayrshire plantocracy was the loss of the 'Carrick' estate on the 'ceded' island of Tobago. Sir Adam Fergusson's youngest brother – James – had set out to make his fortune in the West Indies in 1773 and after a tour of the Leeward and Windward Islands decided to settle on Tobago. This island had been captured thirteen years earlier during the Seven Years Wars and the French planters and their slaves evicted. The Crown had since sold off the vacated lands to speculators, many of whom were soon in difficulties paying their mortgages as it took time and outlay to get a revenue flow of any significance from these stripped and neglected estates.

Without consulting his elder brothers, James made a *very great bargain* by purchasing 300 acres in the Bloody Bay area in the exposed north west of the island from a 'Mr Wilson' for £4,000. His intention was to buy slaves and set them to work planting cotton and indigo. From his projected profits plan he intended to repay his capital outlay in five years.[82]

Inexperienced and working poor soil with his first ten slaves he struggled to establish a viable plantation. He wrote to his brother Charles with a long list of basic necessities that he wanted sent directly to Bloody Bay that included: *two dozen Kilmarnock bonnets, two dozen cutlasses and two dozen course earthenware bowls.*[83] All of which was paid for by Bills of Exchange drawn on his elder brother's account who reluctantly took

---

80   Countess Crawford to James Hunter Blair 6 & 28 April 1782, AA DC 191/ bundle 35.

81   Hugh Hamilton to James Hunter Blair, 21 January 1782, AA DC 191/ bundle 45.

82   NRAS 3572/4/1.

83   NRAS 3572/4/2.

a half share in lieu. James was also aided by his neighbours in Bloody Bay – 'Mr Fullarton', William Bruce and Gilbert Petrie. Indeed, he finally had the estate working as an economically viable concern, just as the war broke out (1776).

In the vanguard of the rebel Americans were their privateers. They infested the Caribbean within months of the first shots being fired on mainland America. Landing and looting remote coastal plantations was the favoured tactic in waging economic warfare against the mother country's interests. These acts drew away British warships from the Continental blockade. While guarding his property James took ill and died (September 1777) aged thirty one. He left behind his legacy - a well established plantation worked by over ninety slaves worth £15,000 sterling.[84]

The year after his death, the inevitable happened. American privateers landed and looted the estate, carrying off equipment and crops and any slaves on which they could lay hands.[85] Worse was to come as the island was devastated by a hurricane in 1780. In the following year the French invaded and, after defeating Governor George Ferguson's militia, occupied the island. On hearing the news, Sir Adam wanted to sell up immediately but this was not an option as there were no buyers whilst the conflict remained unresolved.[86]

After the war, the island was ceded to France by the Treaty of Versailles. 'Memorials' from British owners of plantations on the island addressed to the Prime Minister Lord Shelbourne, unsuccessfully sought compensation.[87] As it transpired their entitlement to their possessions

---

84   NRAS 3572/4/4.

85   The planter neighbour - William Bruce - wrote a lengthy letter to Sir Adam on the raiders who spiked the six-pounder cannon that was meant to deter such landings in the bay. He noted that the buildings on the Carrick estate had been looted but not burned. NRAS 3572/ 4/3.

86   Sir Adam Fergusson to Gilbert Petrie NRAS 3572/4/4.

87   Ibid, NRAS 3572/4/17.

was respected under the peace treaty. But difficulties were placed in their way as they now came under the French colonial *ordonnance* and taxation. In 1785, with little hope of selling the plantation, the Fergussons cut their losses; selling off the slaves and stock to neighbouring planters and leaving the Carrick estate land uncultivated.[88] In 1787 the estate was declare forfeit by the local authorities for non-payment of 'quit rents' and non-cultivation of land; ending that 'unfortunate adventure', as Sir Adam dubbed it.[89]

Peace and Recovery

In Jamaica, the partners held firm during the war and saw out the early market panics largely due to the Houstoun connection that served both the Pemberton Valley and the Rozelle estates. They were soon rewarded as the massive flight of Glasgow 'tobacco lord' capital out of Virginian tobacco and into West Indian sugar drove the price of estates and slaves in Jamaica sky high. As Hugh Hamilton on Pemberton Valley reported: *Such immense prices for estates ... I have at present sixty slaves which would sell for £3,000 sterling. I owe for my last purchase of slaves made in September nearly £1,000 sterling. This from their work I could clear in twelve months.*[90]

Hugh's enthusiasm for slave dealing was not shared by the cash strapped 'Sundrum John' or his aunt the Countess Crawford. They wrote placing an embargo on any new capital outlays at the Pemberton Valley estate. These instructions, however, arrived too late to stop Hugh purchasing new slaves. Hugh was unrepentant on his outlays, as he told Hunter Blair: *Pemberton Valley has for some time past been in very good order which has cost me a good deal of personal fatigue, I by no means regrett it when my constitutents are pleased, but Sundrum was rather peevish in a late letter on my drawing upon him and the Trustees, which it was impossible to avoid, as*

88   Ibid. NRAS 3572/4/9.

89   Ibid. NRAS 3572/4/7 & 11-13.

90   Hugh Hamilton to James Hunter Blair 21 January 1782, AA DC 191/ bundle 45.

I had purchased Slaves prior to the countermanding any future advances on the Estate, which I regularly informed of, had I found the Estate here free of debt, I never would have had occasion to draw for the Negroes I have bought in. We suffer amazingly at present from dry weather I fear much it will shorten our present crops, I apprehend Rozelle must feel it severily. I never was in so bad humour with Jamaica estates as now, the beginning this year I had the most flattering appearance of a great crop and how it will turn out I am now very uncertain.[91]

Undeterred, Hugh worked on clearing the outstanding debts on the Rozelle plantation on behalf of the other partners. At Pemberton Valley his work on the mill dam allowed water to be pumped to the cane fields during the drought the following season (1783). In the meantime, Sundrum encouraged him to clear the estate's outstanding local debts by selling rum on the island to the shippers.

As the conflict wound down and the security situation at sea improved that summer, Hugh decided to come home. Sundrum reckoned that he had accumulated £3000 sterling during his time in Jamaica. This was in addition to the capital locked in the slaves whose ownership he retained. Sundrum John offered to help him settle on his return: *I think I have a good estate for you.* This was Pinmore House in the parish of Colmonel, south of Girvan, and which Hugh bought soon after his arrival back in Ayrshire in 1784. This estate had been previously owned by Robert Kennedy – one of the many victims of the Ayr Bank crash. Hugh fully exploited this situation in his desire to emulate his Uncle Robert's display of success by building his own country park and seat. He seized the moment and bought two plots close by Rozelle House from the insolvent holders of Alloway land from the 1753 roup. These he amalgamated to form his 'Belleisle' Estate raising his new mansion there in 1787.[92]

---

91   Hugh Hamilton to James Hunter Blair, 12 April 1781, AA DC 191/ bundle 35.

92   The plots 'Belleisle west and east' were purchased at the roup by Alexander Campbell, physician, and William Donald, merchant, both of Ayr.

Sandy

Hugh's replacement as manager was his second cousin - Alexander West Hamilton (known as Sandy) - the son of John of Sundrum. Sandy sailed for Jamaica as Hugh's replacement in the summer of 1783. His residency in Jamaica was the longest of any in his family; stretching over twenty years - though interspersed with extended visits home mainly due to health problems.

At the time of his departure a new overseer - Marmaduke Burton - an old sergeant of fifteen years service with the 4th Regiment was sent out to assist him on Pemberton Valley.[93] Burton was expected to deploy his military bearing to handle the slaves with a firm hand. Sandy, holding the Power of Attorney from the trustees, pushed on with the expansion plans first mooted by James Stirling forty years earlier. This involved taking out a seven years lease on a nearby plot - 'Old Toms' - as pasturage to support more cattle and mules to service the Pemberton Valley estate with manure and beasts of burden.[94]

To manage the Rozelle plantation, another relation – John Ferguson of Greenvale – was sent out as factor by the partnership. He was the husband of Robert's second daughter Frances. His overseer was John Gardner, the cousin of Thomas Blane one of the agents in the partners' American ventures.[95] In most correspondence to Hugh back in Ayrshire, Sandy's reports were co-signed by the dominant John Ferguson who was rapidly acquiring a large holding of the new slaves brought onto the estate.

---

93   Burton had a cousin in Jamaica – Dr Hodgson – who was known to the Hamiltons. His indenture was for three years and he was to be paid £20, £25 & £30 for each respective year. He was given £5 and his ticket to Jamaica on account. NAS GD 142/10x.

94   A bullock was usually killed at Christmas to feed the slaves.

95   The Blanes were a Girvan family. Thomas was the main agent in America for the partnership. After the war he tried, unsuccessfully, to recover debts owed to them by tobacco planters. The company storehouse was on the shore of the Yeocomico River, a tributary of the Potomac in Virginia.

Things were progressing well until late August 1785 when a hurricane cut a swathe across north east Jamaica. Port Antonio, the intended destination of the bookkeeper Robert Burns the following year, was devastated with ships sunk in the harbour and wharves demolished. The havoc was such that martial law was declared in the aftermath.

Rozelle escaped fairly lightly but the correspondence at this time also mentions a new joint venture set up by Ferguson and Sandy. This was 'jobbing' out of gangs of Pemberton Valley slaves to work for other plantations – mainly at the Friendship Hall plantation in which Ferguson held an interest.

This lucrative arrangement overstretched the workforce and was soon challenged by Hugh, back in Ayrshire, who found fault with the size and quality of the 1785 sugar crop (165 hogsheads) from the home plantation.[96] There was a further disgruntlement over the rum production levels the following year which raised a serious question mark over the jobbing venture using Pemberton Valley slaves.[97] With a major rift looming over a conflict in interests Hugh had the Kingston attorney - Robert Campbell - undertake a monetary evaluation of the sixty-eight slaves on estate.[98] At the same time their physical condition was also assessed by the plantation surgeon - Dr David Shaw.[99] All of which took its toll on morale of the

---

96   The crop was 165 hogsheads which was lower than that of the neighbouring estates Crescent (175 hhds) and Friendship Hall (175 hhds). John Ferguson to Hugh Hamilton, 25 February 1786, NAS GD 142/2/30. Ferguson may have returned to Jamaica in 1789 but was back in Glasgow by 1790. He died the following year.

97   The collective price put on them was £5425 to which was noted a further five slaves (value £380) belonging exclusively to John Ferguson. An advert dissolving the 'Jobbing Negroes' business with effect from 1 January 1787 was placed in the Kingston newspapers. NAS GD 142/2/65.

98   Robert Campbell apportioned the value of the slaves as follows: £3,000 to Hugh Hamilton, £2005 to Alexander West Hamilton and £1750 to John Ferguson. Dr Shaw reckoned that Sandy needed £1300 to pay off Ferguson. NAS GD 142/2/137-147.

99   Valuation dated 2 January 1786. NAS GD 142/2/6. Shaw owned the 39 acre Bonny Plantation in St Mary's parish which Sandy rented after the doctor's death in 1805. Countess Crawford also held a share on this property.

white staff. In the first half of 1786, the overseer in charge of the boiling house - John Gardner - became 'very ill' and incapable of further service to the estate.

In December of that year, there was considerable upheaval caused by the sudden death of the much trusted overseer at Rozelle - Andrew Murdoch. He had been promoted from bookkeeper to overseer and had carried on the tight reporting of the plantation affairs to the owners - Sir Adam Fergusson and Sir James Hunter Blair –introduced by his predecessor John Paterson.

Archibald Cameron

Holding the fort after Murdoch's demise was the Kingston merchant - Robert McDermert formerly of Straiton, Ayrshire.[100] The first new appointee was a 'Mr Hately' but he was soon replaced as *there was very little planting* done. His replacement was Archibald Cameron who had arrived from Scotland onboard the Houstoun & Company vessel *Castlesemple* back in June 1784. He was, however, not given the position of overseer of the Rozelle estate until mid 1786. It is more than likely that he was not their first choice, as his style of management and reporting was a matter of much concern from the outset.[101] In that unsettling year two more of the young bookkeepers died on the Rozelle plantation reducing the number of whites on the plantation to a critical level set by the 'Deficiency Law'.[102] This regulation demanded that there was, for security reasons, a minimum of one white for every thirty blacks on a plantation.[103]

Arguably, of more consequence to the manner of running the Rozelle

---

100   Robert was the son of the Rev. John McDermott of Straiton. His nephew was bookkeeper for Cruickshank Bailey estate on the island.

101   NRAS 3572/3/7.

102   One was David Dunbar, who died in October, around the same time as Burns would have taken up his position as bookkeeper at Ayr Mount. Dunbar's mother Marion was informed that his will included a gift of money to a local mulatto woman. Ibid.

103   Also one white for every 150 animal stock.

plantation was the death the following year (1787) of one of the owners - Sir James Hunter Blair. His unmarried older brother – Colonel William Hunter now named James' son David, a nine year old, as his inheritor. This brought Hugh Hamilton, one of those appointed to administer the child's interests, back into the circle directing the affairs of Rozelle.

On the north side of the island on the Pemberton Valley plantation, matters came to a head sometime around 1788 with the departure of John Ferguson. He returned to Scotland leaving Sandy Hamilton under a cloud of suspicion with the partners for 'gaming' and soaring personal debts.[104] Even so, with Dr Shaw still close to hand, Sandy was left to manage the estates without a rival to his authority. Over the next few turbulent years he remained the anchor pin, coping with a turnover of personnel.

George Hamilton

Sandy was not without a helper in the daily running of things. One young family member - George Hamilton (who had been under Thomas Blane's tutelage in America) – came over to serve a form of apprenticeship (1789-1800) with him. He proved to be an asset and Sandy was pleased to report back to the partners that he was *doing well, saving money to buy a Negro.*[105] George made a study of the local market for incoming enslaved Africans which was then over-heating in anticipation of Wilberforce's Bill to ban the transatlantic slave trade: *I believe what is commonly asked 'brown children' under ten or twelve is a 'new negro' the best that can be chosen out of a cargo, if they are above that age they are charged at the price of a good seasoned slave which is present from £160 to £200 [island] currency.*[106]

His help was badly needed as there was more trouble brewing on the Rozelle plantation which had been short handed for some time. When Sandy tried to recommend an *old hand under Gardner* – Jack Moore – as

---

104   John Ferguson died in the Glasgow area c.1791.

105   Alexander West Hamilton to Hugh Hamilton, 25 May 1789; NAS GD 142/2/57.

106   George Hamilton to Hugh Hamilton, 19 June 1800; NAS GD 142/2/81.

an assistant overseer to Archibald Cameron, the overseer tried to block the appointment on the grounds that Moore was *lethargic and in an inactive state*.[107] Sandy persevered and, with Sir Adam's support, Moore was taken on but he did not live long in his new position. In 1794 there was a fire, probably wilfully started as two slaves were subsequently 'sold off the island'. Measles also struck, killing a number of the slaves. The acute shortage of white personnel on the estate was particularly felt when the Maroon troubles were at their height and martial law was invoked across the island (1795).[108]

George did well during this emergency and, when Sandy fell ill and had to leave for Scotland (1800), he took over as manager of both estates. But he too succumbed to an illness and was forced to leave for Virginia in August 1801, much to the regret of all the partners. During his last weeks on the island he scoured the local Scots network for a replacement. He identified a 'Mr Donald' as his successor but, not holding the necessary Powers of Attorney to appoint him, he departed leaving the resident overseer - Archibald Cameron – in overall charge of Rozelle.[109]

This left the partners back in Ayrshire with the onerous task of finding a new factor. Captain John Ferguson proposed his nephew for the position - yet another John Ferguson. He had been on the island for eight years and was an old hand at the planter business. Support was forthcoming from Peter Ballantine in Kingston. But Sir Adam Fergusson was wary of entrusting his plantation to such an individual and raised *a very strong objection preferring a man who was in a manner, a stranger to me*. The matter was resolved when it was agreed to appoint Ferguson but with

---

107   Alexander West Hamilton to Hugh Hamilton, 31 May 1793, NAS GD 142/2/75.

108   Series of letters from Archibald Cameron to Sir Adam Fergusson, 13 December 1794, AA DC 191/ bundle 10.

109   Cameron became seriously ill in the aftermath, aggravated by overwork. The despairing owners even considered granting powers of attorney to run the estate to the bookkeeper – Alan Cameron – in the event of his death. Sir Adam Fergusson to Hugh Hamilton, 15 March 1796: AA DC 191/ bundle 11.

'dormant powers'.[110] One major reason for his compromise was that the young Sir David Hunter Blair had reached his maturity and was about to assume control of his own affairs from the trustees, including his half of the Rozelle plantation.

Black Slaves & White Bookkeepers

The annual reports and correspondence sent back to Scotland from the various managers on the plantations stretch over a period of eighty years. Yet they rarely mention the lives of their slaves - other than as prime capital assets listed along with the livestock. Snippets only mark their mortal coming and going. One fatality mentioned was a three week old baby of one of the slaves. This loss to the inventory was immediately balanced by the birth of another to 'Lucky the Maco wench' whose infant was *likely to do well*.[111]

Another fatality noted was the death of 'Quacy' while being marched from Pemberton valley for transportation to Cuba by a 'Mr Fairlie'.[112] The most dramatic example of the punishment of a trouble-maker was that of the slave 'Doctor Caesar' on the Rozelle plantation during Andrew Murdoch's time as overseer. Caesar had been tolerated as a 'black medicine' practitioner while he was compliant and worked in the fields. But things changed dramatically when he assumed the role of 'driver' of the gang (the top position allowed to black slaves) in Murdoch's absence and in defiance of the carpenter Moodie. On his return, Murdoch had Caesar's thumbs whip corded together before giving him two hundred lashes. Caesar then absconded and had a letter written on his behalf which he sent directly to the owners bitterly complaining about his treatment.[113]

---

110   Sir Adam Fergusson to Hugh Hamilton 18 August 1801: NAS GD 142/35/7.

111   Ibid, 10 March 1787: NAS GD 142/2/45. Infant mortality was very high amongst the slaves as there was little post natal care or rest for the mother. Tetanus was the main killer, see: appendix A.

112   Alexander West Hamilton to Hugh Hamilton, 10 January 1787: NAS GD 142/2/44.

113   NRAS 3572/3/6.

Letter from 'Doctor Caesar' signed with an 'X'

Thereafter he was accused of arson and took to stirring up the other slaves to such a degree that he was declared 'dangerous' and permission was granted for him to be 'sold off the island'. He managed, however, to slip away and onto a ship bound for London where he disappeared. Such was his lingering and disruptive influence that rumours of his return to the island dogged the reports of the managers for months to come.[114]

Virtually nothing is said of the lives of the white book-keepers who rarely left the estates. Their co-habitation with female slaves was a taboo subject in polite society and only once referred to in correspondence to the owners. This breach of etiquette was forced upon Cameron by an ongoing quarrel that threatened discipline and destabilised the social order on the estate.

114   RAS 3572/ 3/7.

This *very unpleasant situation* developed in May 1800 when John Ferguson first took up his appointment as the factor of Rozelle. From the outset he was determined to stamp his authority, and prove that full Powers of Attorney should be granted to him. To this end he was determined to sell off the less controllable mulattos on the plantation. This forced the hand of the overseer - Archibald Cameron – who wrote directly to Sir Adam Fergusson asking permit from the owners to buy his pregnant mistress 'Annie' and the four *feral children* she had by him. He offered £100 sterling each for the twenty-eight year old mother and their ten year old child; £50 for each of younger children (ages seven, four and one); and £10 for the expected child – if born alive.

Sir Adam, with no 'hands on' experience of plantation management, turned to Hugh Hamilton: *I must confess I should be inclined to gratify a Man with respect to his own children and their Mother – especially as I suppose the Mother at least will never be much use by her work to the work upon the estate. But in this I should enquire in what you and the other gentlemen who act for Mr Hunter [Blair] determine. Let me know if I shall say anything or let the matter drop.*

Hugh's advice was businesslike - to apply *the rule always observed in Jamaica* – whereby Cameron was given the option of replacing his concubine and their four children with five new prime slaves, at his expense, as the plantation was *under peopled*. Cameron's response was to withdraw his offer. [115]

Predictably, that was not the end of the matter. Five years later the ramifications were still being felt as the denied Annie took to venting her frustration and anger against the black mistress of the estate carpenter Moodie. The trigger this time was Moodie's request to buy their mulatto son so that he might secure manumission for him that would set him free and out of reach of Ferguson. In a flurry of letters Sir Adam struggled to defuse this new situation that he *did not like the complexion of.* So he

---

115   Sir Adam Fergusson to Hugh Hamilton, 12 June 1800, NAS GD 142/35/9.

turned again to Hugh Hamilton for guidance. It was decided that the disruptive Annie should be removed from the plantation to the workhouse in Kingston. As her incarceration incurred a daily charge to the trustees it was then decided to sell her. Ferguson, apparently exploited the situation to extend his authority, asking permission for her to be 'shipped off' the island. Adam was very uncomfortable with this final solution. *Let me know what is really meant by 'shipping off'. I have understood that it meant selling the slave to be shipped off to the Spaniards to be employed in the mines. If this is the meaning, I confess I could not bring my mind to condemn a woman to so horrible a condition. But perhaps I am mistaken in this supposition and I wish to set rightly for.*[116] Her final fate is not known. What is known is that Moodie bought his son's freedom by handing over another prime male slave to Cameron.

The Abolition of the Transatlantic slave trade of 1807

Trouble with the slaves was further fermented by the abolition of the slave trade which raised their expectations for emancipation. The trainee sent out as a possible replacement for Ferguson - John Hamilton - described the ban as *a severe blow to [white] Jamaicans.*[117] Sandy returned to the island in 1812 to wrestle back control. It did not take him long to denounce Ferguson as a manipulative rogue under whose mis-management a number of the Rozelle's slaves had run off. Soon after that Ferguson left the island *clandestinely* taking more slaves with him.[118]

After restoring his authority Sandy had time to develop his own business. An opportunity not to be missed was in renting or managing the estates for absentee landlords who had retired home after the news of the successful black revolt on Haiti (1791) had reached Jamaica. At the height of his sugar empire building (1814) he was acting 'proprietor' of Pemberton

---

116   Ibid, 23 June 1805, NAS GD 152/35/2.

117   George Hamilton to Hugh Hamilton, 19 June 1800. John Hamilton to Hugh Hamilton, April 1807. Both NAS GD 142/2/81.

118   Alexander West Hamilton to Hugh Hamilton, 30 July 1812. NAS GD 142/2/100-5.

Valley and Rozelle, as well as the Cromwell, Tremolesworth, Hunterston, Fontebelle and Bonny Pen plantations. For his onerous duties he paid himself £420 per annum and employed eight overseers and bookkeepers at Pemberton Valley and six at Rozelle. What he made in his leasing business elsewhere is not known. A year later, however, he was scaling back in preparation for his return to Ayrshire.[119]

The Legacy

The end of the Napoleonic Wars (1815) offers a convenient point at which to disengage from the 'Hamiltons in Jamaica' storyline – which continues for another thirty years or so. It must suffice to say that with the emancipation of slavery in the British West Indies (1834) and the abandonment of the insidious apprenticeship system four years later, the Hamilton plantations became increasingly unmanageable and hence unprofitable and were sold or abandoned.[120]

The year 1817 has particular significance for the dynasty. In that year Robert II's inheritance - the Bourtreehill and Rozelle estates in Ayrshire and his half share of the Pemberton Valley plantation in Jamaica - passed to his last surviving daughter Eleanora and her husband Hugh Montgomerie, the 12th Earl of Eglinton. [121] Burns regularly wandered through their great estate at Kilwinning while learning the flax dressing trade at Irvine.

---

119   His management of the large Tremolesworth estate was wound up and the books squared that year, with the exception made for a runaway woman slave who had been missing for several years: *I have heard of her, but have not yet succeeded in getting her laid hold of.* Ibid.

120   It is worth noting that 147,000 women in West Coast Scotland signed a petition to the young Queen Victoria to end this blatant extension to slavery.

121   Jean Countess Crawford died in 1805 (outliving her children none of whom had issue) whereupon the claim passed to her sister Margaret. Margaret was married to Sir John Cathcart of Carleton (died 1785). She died April 1817 without issue so her estates passed on to Eleanora.

Hugh III had died shortly before 1817 without issue and so his legacy - the Pinmore and Rozelle Ayrshire estates - passed onto his favourite relative Sandy (Alexander West Hamilton).[122]   Only the year before Sandy had married Hamilla Montgomerie, his cousin and daughter of Alexander Montgomerie (the brother of Hugh, the husband of Eleanora).[123] John II's legacy - the Sundrum estate and the final share of Pemberton Valley - passed on his death in 1821 to the eldest son of John III.[124]

The Fergussons connection with the Rozelle plantation continued for at least another quarter of a century as Sir Charles Dalrymple Fergusson of Kilkerran bought Hunter Blair's half in 1848.[125] By then, with sugar beet being subsidised in Europe, the sugar business was in rapid and terminal decline throughout the British Caribbean. The timing and circumstances of their eventual disengagement from the plantation is presently unknown.

---

122   Hugh had married Lilian, daughter of James Ritchie of Busbie but there is no mention of her accompanying him to Jamaica or having issue. There is, however, an entry mentioning 'Jane' - described as 'Hugh's daughter' – departing from Jamaica on the *Ruby* sailing for Port Glasgow accompanied by a negro servant called 'Gammetta' in 1785 – a year after Hugh had returned to Ayrshire: NAS GD 142/2/24.

123   For the account books for their continuing share in the profits of Pemberton Valley Plantation, see; NAS GD 3/3/97.

124   John III had no direct Jamaican connection. He took up a career at sea becoming the commander of the East India Company ship *Bombay Castle*.

125   NRAS 3572/10/46.

Chapter 3

Jamaican Bodies - The Oswalds

Of all the Ayrshire plantocrats to imprint on Burns, the Oswalds of Auchencruive - Richard and Mary - were to the fore. His aversion to this couple was long in its distillation. Richard Oswald died in 1784, two years before Burns' intended voyage to Jamaica, and prior to the radicalisation of the Bard's stance on social injustice and inequality. Soon afterwards, Mary, with a reputed income of £10,000 per annum, retired to London and out of Burns' immediate sight.[126]

Richard Oswald by William Denune

Mary Ramsay (Mrs Oswald)
by Johann Zoffany

126   At the height of their wealth, just before the outbreak of the American War of Independence, the Oswalds owned over 100,000 acres of prime land in Scotland, mostly in Ayrshire and Dumfriesshire.

Mary Ramsay Oswald

It was only after her death, four years later that the Bard's indignation was re-ignited. This was occasioned by the famous chance encounter with her funeral cortege as it trundled its way to the family burial vault in St. Quivox church in the depth of a harsh winter. Burns, then an Excise officer, recalled the incident and its impact on him to his literary friend, Dr. John Moore, then in London:

In January last, on my road to Ayrshire, I had put up at Bailie Whigham's, in Sanquhar, the only tolerable inn in the place. The frost was keen, and the grim evening and howling wind were ushering in a night of snow and drift. My horse and I were both much fatigued with the labours of the day, and just as my friend the Bailie and I were bidding defiance to the storm, over a smoking bowl, in wheels the funeral pageantry of the late great Mrs. Oswald, and poor I am forced to brave all the horrors of the tempestuous night, and jade my horse, my young favourite horse, whom I had just christened' Pegasus', twelve miles farther on, through the wildest moors and hills of Ayrshire, to New Cumnock,the next inn. The powers of Poesy and Prose sink under me, when I describe what I felt. Suffice it to say, that when a good fire at New Cumnock had so far recovered my frozen sinews, I sat down and wrote the inclosed ode.

Earlier in the same letter he had sought to prepare Moore for the vitriolic tone of the accompanying poem: *You probably knew her personally, an honour of which I cannot boast; but I spent my early years in the neighbourhood, and among her servants and tenants. I know that she was detested with the most heartfelt cordiality. However, in the particular part of her conduct which roused my poetic wrath, she was much less blameable.*[127] There is nothing in any of his earlier, or indeed later, works that approaches the degree of vilification or damning verdict that he pronounces on *that venerable votary iron avarice and sordid pride*[128] and *Priestess of Mammon*

---

127   Robert Burns to Dr Moore, Ellisland, 23rd March 1789.

128   This was Burns' description of her in his letter to Peter Stuart editor of the London *Morning Star*. Enclosed with the letter was a copy of the *Ode* which Stuart duly published (7 May) under the nom de plume 'Tim Nettle' to avoid a possible libel suite.

in the first two verses:

Ode, Sacred to the Memory of Mrs Oswald of Auchencruive

Dweller in yon dungeon dark,
Hangman of creation, mark!
Who in widow-weeds appears,
Laden with unhonoured years.
Nosing with care a bursting purse,
Baited with many a deadly curse?

Stophe

View the wither'd beldam's face
Can thy keen inspection trace
Aught of Humanity's sweet, melting grace?
Note that eye, 'tis rheum o'erflows-
Pity's flood there never rose.
See those hands, ne'er stretched to save,
Hands that took - but never gave.
Keeper of Mammon's iron chest,
Lo, there she goes, unpitied and unblest
She goes, but not to realms of everlasting rest!

Mrs Frances Anna Dunlop of Craigie, Burns' confidante, later castigated him for this poem which usurped God's judgement: *Are you not a sad wicked creature to send a poor old wife straight to the Devil, because she gave you a ride in a cold night?*

Mary Oswald was the only daughter of the merchant and planter Alexander Ramsay of Aberdeenshire.[129] She was born there in 1719 and taken to Jamaica as a child along with her mother Jean Ferguson.   Alexander

---

129   He was a member of the extensive Laithers family of Aberdeenshire and Banffshire, see: David Hancock, *Citizens of the World* (Cambridge, 1995), p.64.

was highly successful and acquired extensive business interests there, including warehousing and shipping. As a young girl she was introduced to her future husband, Richard Oswald, at a gathering in Kingston held by the Banffshire *Practitioner in Physick and Chiurgery* Alexander Grant of Dalvey.

In 1738 Mary's father died and she accompanied her mother to London where they resettled. Sometime after the '45 Rebellion crisis subsided, Mary renewed her acquaintance with Richard Oswald in London and they married at St. Martins-in-the-Field on 12 November 1750.[130] She was then thirty one and he was forty five years old.[131] It was a most advantageous marriage for Oswald as her dowry was an inheritance of some £20,000, mainly in property and plantations in Jamaica and southern mainland America. In business terms, the connections he gained through her trustees and family network in western Jamaica were further major assets to the business portfolio of this aspiring man.

Richard Oswald

Richard was of the classic mould of early eighteenth Scottish entrepreneurs, as were his equally avaricious business associates. Born in 1705, he was the second son of the Rev. George Oswald of Dunnet, Caithness.[132] Around the age of twenty he joined his cousins, Richard and Alexander, as a trainee in their counting house in Old Green, Glasgow.[133] They were then expanding their tobacco and sugar business and had extensive interests in the Europe, America and the West Indies.[134] Cousin Richard was, almost

---

130   John Cathcart to Robert Hamilton, 1 December 1750 quoted: ibid, p.246.

131   Richard had two sons – George and Richard - by Agnes Barr of Glasgow who he openly acknowledged and supported. Richard Alexander referred to Mary as 'Mrs Oswald' in his letters to his father.

132   He was pursuing his claim to Skaill lands in Caithness late into his life.

133   Cousins Richard (1687-1762) and Alexander (1694-1763) had business dealings with James and Robert Stirling of Keir in Jamaica.

134   Young Richard was sent out as a 'super cargo' on a number of voyages to America and the West Indies and also resided in Virginia for six years.

certainly, involved in the Clyde's ventures in the transatlantic slave trade around this time as he was called on as the 'expert witness' on 'the trade' during a prolonged legal dispute heard at Edinburgh.[135]

Making profits out of the endemic warfare of the eighteenth century was Richard's particular forte. Luck smiled on him (and his cousins) during the War of Austrian Succession 1744-9 when one of their armed traders carrying 'letters of marque' took a rich incoming French prize off Ireland during the early months of the war.

His share of this windfall and the profits of diligent trading, bankrolled his move to London where he set up in business for himself in 1745. By the time he married Mary, five years later, he was deeply embedded in the circle of Scots traders in London and already comfortably well off.[136] Three years further on, and backed by her money, he took the biggest gamble of his career. This was to buy, with his close associates, the derelict slaving fortress on Bance Island

in the estuary of the Sierra Leone River in West Africa. It had been abandoned by Royal Africa Company (RAC) in the 1728s after being successively looted and burnt by pirates, French privateers and, finally, local Africans.[137]

Bance Island Slaving Fort, Sierra Leone by unknown artist.

---

135   See: Eric J Graham, 'The Slaving Voyage of the *Hannover* of Port Glasgow 1719-20' *History Scotland* (Vol. 3, No.5, September 2003), pp.26-34.

136   Of the five in his inner circle, four had Scottish connections: Alexander Grant of Dalvey, Augustus and John Boyd (from Northern Ireland and St. Kitts and closely related to the 'Kilmarnock Boyds') and John Mill of Montrose. The rise of Oswald and his associates and their ventures is comprehensively reviewed in Hancock's, *Citizens of the World* (Cambridge, 1995).

137   Eric J Graham, *Seawolves: Pirates & the Scots* (Edinburgh, 2005).

It was a gamble that promised to pay off handsomely as the African Trade Act of 1750 stripped the old malfunctioning RAC of its monopoly. Its forts, with the exception of Bance Island, was given to a new company and the slave carrying trade thrown open to independent traders. It was not, however, until 1752 that Grant, Oswald & Company were confirmed in their ownership of the fort. Over the next ten years they expended inordinate amounts of money rebuilding and fortifying the fortress and its slave compounds.[138]

In the meantime another other of Richard's schemes fell into place, no doubt also underpinned by Mary's inheritance. This was securing the lucrative contract to provide bread and provisions for the armies fighting under the Duke of Brunswick in Europe during the Seven years War (1756-63). This business earned him the label *Plunderer of Armies* from Burns.[139]

By the end of the war and the commissary contract, the Oswalds were back in Britain and flush with money.[140] In July 1764 they acquired from James Murray, a business connection, the Auchencruive estate, five miles inland on the banks of the River Ayr. The mansion house designed by Robert Adam was then incomplete and it took the Oswalds three years to finish it. Richard, mostly in London tending to his extensive business affairs, relied heavily on his factor John Maxwell to supervise the builders. Plainly a task with which Maxwell was uncomfortable with: *The whole work in your new house goes on very slowly and in short I have no pleasure in looking at what is done and adoing. I do wish and entreat that you could find some more able person to direct and conduct the execution of the work on the principal storey so that you may have some comfort in the possessing of it.*[141]

---

138   A Swedish botanist, Smeathman, visiting the island in 1773 noted a golf course with tartan clad slave caddies, as quoted in Hancock, *Citizens of the World*, p.3.

139   First line in the penultimate verse of his *Ode to the Sacred Memory to Mrs Oswald*.

140   Mary had been in Germany close by Richard as he supervised his commissariat contract. For her letters to him, see; NAS GD 213/52.

141   Letter from John Maxwell to Richard Oswald 1767; NAS GD 213/54/39.

Auchencruive House with first additional wing c.1770.

Over the next two decades the Oswalds lavished vast amounts of money on their Ayrshire estate; adding wings, more outbuildings and filling the house and gardens with fine art.[142]   All of which the young Burns and his family would have been painfully aware, as they struggled to make a living.

In local matters the Oswald were conspicuous as the principal heritor owning two thirds of the small parish of St. Quivox. On their arrival they appointed to the living a young minister straight from his ordination at St. Andrews – the Rev. Mr. William McQuhae. [143] Burns later knew the renowned McQuhae 'the Divine' as the local leader of the 'new lichts' in the West of Scotland, poking fun at him in *The Twa Dogs* (1787) in which he is referred to as *that curs'd rascal ca'd McQuhae.*

---

142   The most impressive building being the Robert Adam garden 'tea house ' built in 1778.

143   McQuhae was born in Wigton 1737 and educated at Glasgow University. He was tutor to the children of, and close friend of the abolitionist James Boswell of Auchinleck prior to being ordained and installed as minister of St Quivox in March 1764. Author of *Difficulties which Attend the Practice of Religion No Just Argument Against It,* he has been referred to as the 'father of the synod'.

Drawing of Burns by William McQuhae junior

Aided by the other heritors, the Oswalds refurbished the local church and crypt and added, at their own expense, a new aisle in 1767. By which time McQuhae had commenced to rebuild the old St. Quivox manse in a grand style for himself and his rapidly expanding family.[144]   A clue as to where the minister found the funds to do so may lie in the fact that his eldest son Richard died on the family owned plantation of Two Mile River in the parish of St. Catherine's Jamaica in 1805.[145]

It was prior to the acquisition of the Auchencruive estate that Richard and his associates in London fully developed their prime asset - the slaving factory on Bance Island in the mouth of the Sierra Leone River. Yet again it was the Seven years War that provided the lift off. Business opportunities abounded following the spectacular British military successes against

---

144   William married Elizabeth, daughter of William Park of Barkip (Beith) physician by whom she had seven children. She died in 1780 and William two years later married Mary Laurie by whom he had a further eight children.

145   Two of William's children by his first marriage - the Rev. Stair McQuhae of St Quivox and Charles (female) McQuhae, wife of William McDowall - claimed the compensation for the 102 slaves on the estate (£2114-15/9d) in 1836. *Legacies of British Slave ownership* database: http://www.ucl.ac.uk/lbs/search/.

the French in India, North America and the West Indies.[146] In the latter theatre, the islands of St Vincent, Grenada, Tobago and Dominica were captured. These were then 'ceded' to the British Crown by the Treaty of Versailles and the French planters vacated along with their slaves. This sparked a land grab on the 'ceded islands' and a rush to re-stock these new possessions with slaves who would be driven hard to quickly generate income to pay back mortgages.

To manage this upsurge in demand for new 'salt water' African slaves, Richard and his associates hired young Scottish lads to go out to Bance Island as bookkeepers.[147] Over the next fifteen years they processed over 12,000 enslaved Africans through the fortress. Many were carried on vessels belong to his firm Oswald, Grant & Company whose counting house was in Philpot Lane, London. As often as not, they were delivered to fellow Scots in the West Indies or America.

Richard's main receiving agent on mainland America was Henry Laurens in Charleston. This town was then the main conduit for slaves passed on to the extremely unhealthy rice fields in the immediate

TO BE SOLD. on board the Ship *Bance-Island*, on tuesday the 6th of *May* next, at *Ashley-Ferry*; a choice cargo of about 250 fine healthy

NEGROES,

just arrived from the Windward & Rice Coast.
—The utmost care has already been taken, and shall be continued, to keep them free from the least danger of being infected with the SMALL-POX, no boat having been on board, and all other communication with people from *Charles-Town* prevented.
Austin, Laurens, & Appleby.

N. B. Full one Half of the above Negroes have had the SMALL-POX in their own Country.

Charleston advertisement of sale of slaves from Bance Island.

---

146   Richard's cousins sent out their crack ship the *Achilles* of Port Glasgow as a privateer, see: Eric J Graham, *A Maritime History of Scotland 1650-1790* (East Linton, 2002) p. 226.

147   One was James Low 'late of Scotland' whose three year indenture was signed in August 1761. He was entitled to *bed, board and washing* and a free passage back home, either directly or via the West Indies. His initial annual salary was £20, increasing by £5 each year thereafter. He was given an advance of £10 on arrival in London; NAS GD 345/1180 bundle 66.

hinterland and the cotton and indigo plantations further south in Georgia and Florida. The pressing need in the 1750s was for full cargoes of healthy slaves, rather than the disease ravaged cargoes that were reaching Charleston at the time on the slavers that had spent months at different forts along the Guinea Coast. As the Aberdeenshire born Charleston physician Dr Garden observed: *There are few ships that come here from Africa but have many of their Cargoes thrown overboard; some one-fourth, some one-third, some lost half; and I have seen some that have lost two thirds of their slaves, I have often gone to visit those Vessels on first Arrival, in order to make a Report to the Governor and Council, but I have never yet been onboard one that did not smell most offensive and noisome, what for Filth, putrid Air; putrid Dysentries (which is their common Disorder) it is a wonder than any escape with Life.*[148]

Henry Laurens as 5th President.

Bance Island slaves were, therefore, highly sought after as they arrived with a much lower incidence of disease onboard having been collected in one up lift and conveyed directly to Charleston.[149] Laurens was also on hand to oversee their passing on by sea to the ports of Savannah, Georgia and St. Augustine in East Florida.

---

148   Letter from Dr Garden to Stephen Hales, as quoted in: *Dr Alexander Garden of Charles Town* (Chapel Hill, 1969), p. 124.

149   As Laurens informed Oswald on 29 June 1756, that his sloop – the *Carlisle* – Captain Osborn had arrived in Charleston with 141 slaves from the factory having lost only five in the 'middle passage'; Elizabeth Donan, *Documents Illustrative of the History of the Slave Trade*, Vol. IV, (Washington, 1935) item no 214, p. 214.

While Oswald's business acumen was renowned, he did commit one gross error of judgement when he purchased a vast unseen tract of land (20,000 acres) in East Florida. Much of it was swamp only suitable for rice planting. The centrepiece was his Timoka plantation on which he had 230 slaves labouring to grow sugar cane - aided by crushing mill machinery shipped from Britain – with little return.

Back in Ayrshire he cultivated various varieties of sugar cane in glasshouses on his Auchencruive estate, the seeds from which he sent to Florida.[150] It was not until 1779 that he gave up on his sugar crop experiments at Timoka and allowed the planting of rice. At the end of the American War of Independence, Florida was ceded back to Spain as part of the peace treaty which Oswald was so instrumental in brokering.[151]   He received compensation for his loss but this still left the Florida plantation scheme with large losses which his great nephew and heir Richard Alexander Oswald put at nearly £15,000.

Richard Alexander Oswald

When Mary Oswald died in 1788 without issue Richard Alexander Oswald, a great nephew of her husband, inherited the Auchenharvie estate. He had already inherited his father's grand estate of Scotstoun in the outskirts of Glasgow. The young rich Richard Alexander appears to have been a sufficiently different animal to his avaricious father and uncles to persuade Burns to set aside his distaste for the Oswalds:

---

150   He even imported Spanish mules – which were highly reckoned as pack animals in the West Indies – into Ayrshire. An odd innovation since Richard was so active in setting up turnpikes and road improvement in Ayrshire. The local farmers were not interested and stuck with their preference for draught horses suitable for ploughing the heavy Ayrshire soil or carting; Hancock , *Citizens of the World*, p. 163.

151   Oswald was sent to Paris by the British government to meet with the American Ambassador - Benjamin Franklin – to strike a deal that would extract Britain from a war she could not win and which had drawn in most of her European rivals. For this service he is known in history as the 'Peace Maker' rather than a slave trader.

An' there'll be wealthy young Richard,
Dame Fortune should hang by his neck
But for prodigal thriftless bestowing,
His merit had won him respect.

Burns was easily won over by Richard's first wife and celebrated beauty Louisa 'Lucy' Johnstone.[152] He was sufficiently enamoured by *that incomparable woman* to change the dedication of *O Wat Ye Wha's in Yon Town* from Jean Lorimer to her in May 1795. She died young, the year after Burns, while seeking respite from her consumption in Lisbon, leaving Richard with two infants.

Mrs Richard Alexander Oswald
by Henry Raeburn.

In 1817, he re-married. His new wife was the widow Lady Lilias Montgomerie, daughter of the twelfth Earl of Eglinton and Eleanora Hamilton.[153] Such was the tight circle of the elite of Ayrshire at the time.

Lilias Montgomerie with grandson Archiblad Hamilton by unknown artist. Courtsey of the MacLaurin Trust

---

152   Daughter of Wayne Johnstone of Hilton in the Merse, she was an accomplished dancer and a talented composer of tunes, some of which were published by the celebrated fiddler-composer Neil Gow.

153   Her first husband was the much reviled persecutor of radicals – Law Lord Robert Dundas MacQueen of Braxfield. He had died in 1799.

Chapter 4

St. Kitts Bodies - The Cunynghams

North Ayrshire was home ground to the Cunynghams of Glengarnock and Cayon, St Kitts.[154]   While sufficiently removed from Burns' immediate locality to be out of his immediate sight, they were interconnected to the principal South Ayrshire and Renfrewshire sugar plantocrats.

Cunyngham of Cayon Coat of Arms

Robert

Robert, the founder of the sugar dynasty, was born in March 1669, the seventh son of Richard Cunyngham of Glengarnock, in the parish of Kilbirnie, Ayrshire.[155]   Robert's reckless father died the following year, leaving a wife and twelve children with crippling debts from his disastrous

---

154   A shorter non-referenced version of this section was published in *History Scotland* as 'Sugar Plantocrats – the Cunynghams of Glengarnock and Cayon St.Kitts' Vol. 7 No.8 (November, 2007).

155   The Glengarnock estate with ruined castle was once part of the Robertland estate in the parish of Kilbirnie. Robertland was home to the Hunter family mentioned in the chapter on the Hamiltons. See: George Robertson, *A Genealogical Account of the Principal Families in Ayrshire more particularly in Cunninghame* (Edinburgh, 1823) Vol. I, 313-318. The spelling of 'Cunyngham' changes over time to 'Cuningham' and finally 'Cunningham'.

military escapades during the Civil War.[156] The eldest son Richard II duly inherited the Glengarnock estate but was forced to sell it whilst Robert was still an infant. The family fortunes were only partly restored when his elder brother married the heiress of Baidland - an estate further down the Garnock Valley above Dalry.

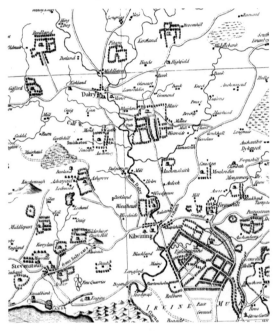

With little hope of rapid advancement at home, the teenage Robert was encouraged by his aunt, Lady Janet Cunyngham of Craigends in Renfrewshire, to follow his next brother up William to seek his fortune in the West Indies.[157] William was a drunkard who had reneged on his apprenticeship with a Glasgow merchant. Indeed, his family had to ask for his indenture fee back so that he could leave Scotland with some start-up trade goods. He finally left with a bundle of linens, most of which he

Detail of Armstrong's 1775 Map of Ayrshire showing Baidland, Broomhill, Kilbirnie House estates and ruins of Glengarnock Castle.

---

156   Richard, like his father before him, was an ardent royalist who raised, at his own expense, a troop of horse for the Crown during the 'Engagement' serving under the Duke of Hamilton. He was captured at the Battle of Preston (1641) and paroled to the Kirk of Kilbirnie. He rode out again for the Crown during the Civil War and was captured at the Battle of Worcester (1651). He was never recompensed for his outlays after the Restoration.

157   He later questioned her motives as she had acquired property that he later reckoned should have been part of his father's estate when he died. Both her sons went to Jamaica where they married heiresses. One died c.1743 and the other c.1745. After which the Stirlings (Robert and James) managed their plantations for the 'ladies'[widows]. One was sold to pay off debts to Robert Stirling in 1748.

sold and squandered on drink when his ship called into Dublin en route. What was left of his trading stock went the same way soon after he landed on St. Christopher (universally referred to as St. Kitts) one of the Leeward Islands.[158]

This small island, just five miles across by seven long, was then known as the 'Garden of the Caribbean' due to the high fertility of its volcanic soils and the abundance of streams. There had been a Scottish presence on the island as far back as 1644 when merchant adventurers from the port of Ayr first arrived to trade for tobacco and sugar.[159] At the time of the Cunyngham brothers arrival (sometime around 1685) the ownership of plantations on the island was split between French planters on the northern half (Capesterre) and the English planters to the south (Basseterre) with the salt pans on the southern isthmus shared.

In his journal, Robert states that, having arrived virtually penniless, he took a position as a bookkeeper to a local merchant eventually earning £70 per year. Most of which he spent rescuing his wastrel brother from penury. William, unfortunately, proved to be a long term liability to Robert, with a wife and five young children to support. Robert gave him £100 to start afresh in North America but the proverbial 'bad penny' was back as soon as the money ran out. Robert, however, refused to bail him out again: *I had done a kind brother part, and would do no more.* This experience gave him an aversion to drink for the rest of his life.

Like so many young Scots, Robert's first step up the social ladder of the plantocracy was due to war. The Protestant 'Glorious Revolution of 1688' created the Jacobite threat overnight and sparked the 'Second Hundred Years War' with their main supporter - Catholic France. Caught in the middle were the Protestant French Huguenots who had previously fled to St. Kitts following the persecution of the Edict of Nantes (1682).

---

158   NAS CS 96/3096/1.

159   See: Barclay & Graham, *Early Transatlantic Trade of Ayr.*

As the conflict spread to the Caribbean, St. Kitts fell to a French expedition from Martinique and was occupied for a short time during the summer of 1689. The arrival of Duke of Bolton's Regiment of Foot from England quickly restored the status quo on the island. Robert states that he felt compelled, *as a gentleman*, to enlist as an Ensign in this regiment. He acquitted himself well and rose to the rank of Captain during the forlorn attempt to capture the key French island of Guadaloupe in 1693.

On his return to St. Kitts, his regiment was disbanded and he settled to the life of a planter, renting the Cayon estate. In late September of that year he married Judith Elizabeth de Bonnefant, a well connected high-born French Huguenot. This union was the making of him as she was the favoured niece of Elizabeth de Salenave, widow of Jordain de Salenave, a major planter on the island.[160]

Over the next ten years Robert consolidated his skills in running the Cayon sugar plantation In the census taken on the island in January 1708, the thirty-eight year old was recorded as head of an extensive family (he had fifteen children by his first wife, of whom eight survived to adulthood) and owned seventy enslaved Africans and Creoles. [161]

Being a renting planter was not an easy path to wealth and security. As a member of the island's ruling council, he was imprisoned for refusing to endorse a 'gift' of £150,000 (island currency) to the rapacious Governor Walter Douglas.[162] This was followed by major problems over his wife's

---

160   See: *Caribbeana* Vol. I (1909), pp.100-102. Also James Paterson, *History of the County of Ayr* (Edinburgh, 1852) Vol. II, pp, 120-1. Judith's father was Daniel de Bonnefont of Martas, her mother was Mary de Barat, sister of Charles de Barat, Sieur De La Bodie, Lt. General to the King of France and Governor of Lisle in Flanders. He was shot dead by a British soldier trying to cross the lines to reach the British garrison during the French siege of St Kitts in 1689.

161   His extensive ledgers, day books and waste books were lodged with the Court of Session and provide the bulk of the information that follows: NAS CS 96/3096-3106.

162   Douglas of Bads had been made a burgess of Glasgow in November 1712. He was removed from office for 'Male Administraion' and sentenced to five years and fined £500 in 1716. I am very grateful to Mark Duffill for this information and what follows on the Cunyngham's legal battles through the English Courts.

inheritance. Elizabeth's aunt died in London in early 1715. By her will Elizabeth stood to inherit the large 'Morning Star' plantation (just under 400 acres) in the northern French dominated St. John's parish. It was not to be a straightforward transference of ownership. By the Treaty of Utrecht (1713) Louis conceded all French claims to St. Kitts, whereupon those French planters who had assisted the invaders were expelled to St. Dominigue and their lands confiscated. During this upheaval a number of estates owned by Protestant Huguenots, despite remaining loyal to the British Crown, were usurped by officials - one being the De Salenave plantation.

In 1717 Robert thought it necessary to travel to London to expedite matters. It proved to be a prolonged fight through the courts which kept him there for two years. During his time in London he made himself indispensable to important people back on St. Kitts; settling bills for Governor Douglas' wife and arranging shipment of everything from coal to books (he sent over a thousand titles) to the island. It was during this sojourn that he connected with the Scottish trading community in London and the merchant William Coleman through whom he would conduct most of his business in sugar.

Elizabeth's claim to the De Salenave plantation was ultimately restored by an Order in Council in 1721.[163] Robert, confident in the eventual outcome, had long since returned to St. Kitts. Using his wife's future inheritance as security, he purchased the Cayon estate that he been renting since 1693, and took over the running of another plantation on the neighbouring island of Nevis from the widow of Colonel Bartholomew Rees on payment of an annuity of £100 to her.[164] From his extensive business ledgers it is clear he immediately utilised his London connections to conduct

---

163   Letters Patent by King George I to Robert Cunningham granted 30 September 1721: British Library MS Eg/ Ch/ 7381. The neighbouring planter, Mr Spooner, lodged caveats contesting the ownership of a segment of the Salenave estate.

164   In an entry in his journal (30 January 1734) he notes: *My negro woman Bathia bore a Mulatto Son. Bat Rees* – implying that the Colonel was the father.

business on behalf of a number of Huguenot and British planters. He also managed the affairs of a succession of local governors who, like Douglas, were fellow Scots.

The Neighbours

Under their governorship St. Kitts became an established 'Scots Lot'. Robert's neighbours and his oftimes business partners on the island were Major James Milliken, Colonel William McDowall, Judge John Greatheed, Augustus Boyd, Robert Colhoun and James Gordon.[165] In a replay of Robert's ascent to the plantocracy, James Milliken came by his war-ravaged plantation on the island of Nevis by marrying Mary Stephen - the widow of Richard Tovey. Through her, James directly benefited from the dowager Tovey's will when she died in 1715. Six years later, the Millikens relocated to St. Kitts. They acquired the 'Monkey Hill' Plantation behind the town of Basseterre, from the great sell-off of French property confiscated by the Crown.

Bassaterre St. Kitts with Monkey Hill and Canada Hills in the background

James' militia commander, Colonel William McDowall, followed suite by marrying James' step daughter, also called Mary. This union also received the blessing of the matriarch Tovey in her will. The McDowalls bought a 200 acre lot at the sale close to Cayon Plantation. Augustus Boyd acquired

---

165 The military ranks may well have been militia titles. Augustus Boyd came out from Northern Ireland and was related to the Boyd's of Kilmarnock who had taken up a 'plantation' there. A branch of the Cunynghames had done the same – settling at Springhill, near Moneymore, Londonderry.

50 acres to add to the two plantations his father-in-law, a prominent judge on the island, put his way after he married his daughter. Boyd later moved to London where he formed his own circle and joined forces with Richard Oswald of Auchencruive and Alexander Grant of Dalvey to purchase the slaving fort on Bance Island, Sierra Leone.

Not all of Cunyngham's associates prospered so easily. Greatheed was ousted from his position as Chief Justice on the island while James Gordon was ruined by a charge of rape of a white woman. Robert Colhoun does not seem to have found a plantation owning widow to marry thereby limiting his progress in St. Kittian society.

The Golden Age of Sugar

Prior to Robert's retirement the sugar business was - hurricanes and droughts permitting – booming. Indeed, output on St. Kitts had increased five fold in the twenty years since he first settled.[166] By 1723 he felt that his plantations were in sufficient order, under his new overseer John Rhodes and his sons, to return to London. He took with him two black slave boys, 'Jack' and 'Phenix' as valets. While in London he had silver slave collars made for them as a symbol of his wealth as a successful planter.[167] His primary reason for this visit was to manage the Crowland estate of Major General Hunter, the new Governor of Jamaica. It was meant to be a short stay but a bad fall from a horse that November kept him longer than he had planned. On his return to St. Kitts this injury was further aggravated and he was forced to return to London for treatment *at great expense*. It was during this second absence that his neighbour, the new Chief Justice on the island - John Spooner - seized over ninety acres of

---

166   For an overview of trading conditions and prices see: Richard Sheridan, *Sugar and Slavery: an economic history of the British West Indies* (Barbados, 1974).

167   They were made by the silversmith James Currie of London and cost £9.14/-. Their livery costumes cost less at £8.10/6 : NAS CS 96/ See also: Eric J Graham, 'Black People in Scotland during the Slavery Era', *Scottish Local History* (issue 71, 2007) pp. 11-16.

Cunyngham property by *clandestine depositions*.[168] On Robert's return (1727) he commenced a legal action to recover his land. Given the legal expertise and position of his opponent, it was probably inevitable that Robert lost the case - incurring £3000 in legal costs in the process.[169]

By then Robert had strengthened his social position in planter society by the advantageous marriage of two of his daughters – Mary and Susanna. Mary married Isaac Roberdeau in 1723, the son of a Huguenot planter on the west side of the island.[170] Susanna married Samuel Mackinnen, sometime around 1725, youngest son of the Aberdeen-born Doctor Daniel Mackinnen, a well established planter on Antigua.[171]

During the early 1730s sugar prices in London slipped back catching the speculating Robert over-exposed. In characteristic fashion his response was to move up the 'food chain' by investing in the production of rum. This involved building a new windmill (to crush the sugar cane) and a fire-resistant boiling house with six copper pans inside. The 'know-how' of distilling he cribbed from his son-in-law's father Daniel Mackinnen. The island's 1733 census notes his major leap forward as a planter; now owning 235 slaves and a property in Basseterre.[172] A year later, by his own accounts, he had increased his work force by 50 more new slaves and was clearing scrub land for a new plantation on the side of Brimstone

---

168   An Order in Council in June 1726 replaced his 1721 grant to the Salenave plantation. Excluded was Spooner's squatter claim made in 1724 to 93 prime acres of Salenave land. NAS CS 96/3102 .

169   It would appear that Robert was eventually compensated with 94 acres of Crown land on the other side of the estate.

170   The descendants of Robert's daughter Mary have made their mark in American History. Her son Daniel Roberdeau (born on St. Kitts in 1722 before she moved to Philadelphia) was a great patriot and a famous general during the American War of Independence. One of his descendents is wife of ex-President George W. Bush. See: 'Cunynham and Roberdeau of St. Kitts', *Caribbeana* Vol.5, pp. 173-6.

171   See: 'Mackinnen of Antigua and St Kitts', *Caribbeana* Vol.4, pp 241-2. Samuel inherited £1000 and settled in St. Kitts by 1725.

172   List dated 25 December 1733.

Mountain - one of St. Kitts two peaks.[173] He hired another overseer – Mr Monck – for this arduous project but sacked him six months later for *not keeping my negroes at their work.*

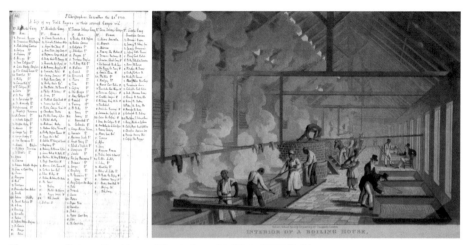

Slave gang list on the Cayon Plantation. St. Kitts 1733 (left).
Interior of a boiling house by William Clark (right).

In that year he undertook the management of Colonel McDowall's plantation when McDowall left the island to develop his great Castlesemple estate on the banks of Lochwinnoch, Renfrewshire in 1727. To do this, Robert put in a manager, John Thompson, with an accountant, 'Mr Alexander', who did the 'books' which Robert inspected before they were sent to Scotland.[174]

These were the good years. Robert's married daughters shuttled between St. Kitts, Antigua and Philadelphia on extended social visits. At home on his Cayon Plantation he busied himself planting numerous shrubs

---

173   Journal dated 6 February 1734.

174   McDowall also retrieved his family seat of Garthland in Galloway from a cousin and bought and restored Shawfield House in central Glasgow. His business partner Major Milliken acquired a neighbouring estate in Johnstone which he named 'Milliken Park'. Both remained active and were involved in shipping hogshead sugar to their 'sugarries' in Glasgow and Leith. Their children founded the great West Indies trading house of Alexander Houstoun & Company.

and indulged his grand daughters by giving them new born heifers and slave servants. In 1734 he felt the need to write down the members of his household which included his long term white servant Daniel Robinson. Robert noted his death with regret in his day book, a sentiment that he never wasted on his slaves. Their deaths he catalogued beside that of his horses and cows, noting only what killed them. The exception was new born infants, most of whom never survived more than a few days, due to the lack of post natal care and tetanus. In their case he listed the slave parents, without further comment, to mark their brief time on earth.

He also invested in the delivery side of the business buying an eighth share in an ocean-going vessel - the *William & Ann*. She joined the other regular ships on which he took cargo space: the *Mary* (Captain David McDowall), the *McDowall* (Captain Thomas Milliken), *St. Andrew* (Captain John Brown) and the *Prince of Orange* (a replacement for the *Mary*). Most sailed with sugar consigned to his London agent - William Coleman. One per year, usually the *St. Andrew,* headed for Port Glasgow with a cargo for William McDowall's 'sugarrie'.[175]

Price List of the 'St. Christopher Sugarrie', High Street, Edinburgh.

Not all Robert's ventures went smoothly. In 1734 agents for the Widow Rees took legal action against him. They claimed that he had mismanaged her Nevis plantation for his own ends and that

---

175   For shipment list from St. Kitts, see: NAS CS 96/3106.

her annuity of £100 was grossly inadequate. In pursuit of these claims they seized nine of his mules and took away a slave woman. To check their excesses Robert sent his son Charles to Monserrat to represent him in court. The cost of which was covered by an ever-increasing mortgage held by his London agent Coleman (£3,000 by the time he left St. Kitts).

Daniel Cunyngham

Daniel Cunyngham by Chamberlain Mason. Courtsey of the Courtauld Institute (left). Elizabeth, Mrs Daniel Cunyngham by Allan Ramsay. Courtesy of the National Portrait Gallery of Scotland (right).

It was always Robert's intention (he was then a widower) to retire back to Ayrshire leaving his estates in the hands of his sons – Richard, Daniel and Charles. Daniel was by far the most active of the sons and with the perfect attributes to do well in St. Kitts society. Sometime around 1733 he had married Elizabeth, the daughter of Anthony Hodges - a planter in the parish of St. Peters who had once been the Deputy Governor of the neighbouring island of Monserrat.[176] Socially, they were an ideal match. Daniel was in his early thirties and acting manager, assisted by his younger brother Charles, of his family holdings. The 'jewel in the crown' was their Cayon Plantation in the parish of St. Mary.

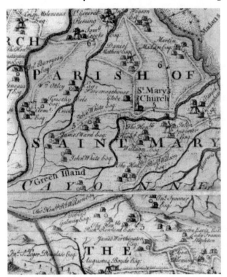

Detail from Bakers 1753 map of St Kitts showing plantations of Daniel Cunyngham and Augustus Boyd.

In the summer of 1737 Robert sailed home. He had planned a very comfortable retirement having bought from his elder brother the Baidland estate in Dalry, close to the old family seat of Glengarnock. He then added to his property portfolio in Ayrshire: Ashenyard (Ashgrove) House in nearby Kilwinning and the Craig estate in Kilmaurs (which he renamed 'Cunyngham's Rest'). In addition, he was to receive the princely sum of £2,500 (£200,000 today's value) annually from the plantation revenues.

For a while the sons worked together to maintain the various holdings and meet their obligations. This allowed Daniel and his wife the opportunity to visit London (1740-1) where Elizabeth had her portrait painted by Allan Ramsay.[177]

On their return, however, Daniel took sole control of the family business

---

176   It would appear that they married in Philadelphia, the new home of Daniel's married elder sister - Mrs Mary Roberdeau. Their voyage home with their first child (July 1734) was a perilous one, as their ship was wrecked on shoals off Barbados and they had to be rescued.

177   This magnificent portrait entitled *Elizabeth, wife of Daniel Cunyngham* now hangs in the dining room of Duff House, Banffshire.

as his elder brother Richard was either unwilling or in too poor health to maintain his role. He also took up his father's place on the ruling council on the island (1741-2) cementing his status with his planter peers. As fate would have it, the elder brother died in July 1743, leaving Daniel as the heir apparent. He did not have to wait long as, four months later, his seventy-four year old father died and was buried in Greyfriars, Edinburgh. However, what seemed to be a secure position was soon to be set on its head by events in Scotland.

Mary Gainer

When his elderly father stepped ashore at London he was a wealthy man and took a house keeper - Mary Gainer. She was then forty years his junior and a mother of four children by a liaison with a Scottish army officer - Captain James Dalrymple. Dalrymple had recently dumped her and their children with a small allowance in Edinburgh that April when he married a 'Miss Cunningham'. Gainer was not at all pleased with this arrangement and took her children off to London *to continue her old Trade*, as Dalrymple put it. In a matter of weeks she had found a new champion and protector - Robert Cunyngham.

The Process of Scandal

Robert brought her back to Edinburgh in 1739 as his house keeper. They immediately put it about in polite circles that Captain Dalrymple was a bigamist – being still legally married to Mary – and a rogue who had abandoned her and their children for a more advantageous union. Such an accusation was not to be tolerated in Georgian society and in September of that year Dalrymple brought a 'Process of Defamation' against her. With Robert's help, she retaliated with 'Declarator of Marriage and Legitimacy' that November. In this document she claimed that she had been abducted and confined by Dalrymple after a regimental ball in Kilkenny in 1723. Trapped, she only agreed to his advances if they were married. This ceremony was duly conducted by a Catholic priest in front of witnesses.

For his part, Dalrymple readily admitted that she had been his mistress, following him under the cover of his 'house keeper' on his postings abroad to Gibraltar and Port Mohan Minorca, and that he was the father of her four children. But he strenuously denied that he had ever married her. To support his claim he produced testimonies from a succession of fellow officers from the time of the Kilkenny posting who testified that she was a well known Irish *woman of pleasure* turned camp follower. All swore that they had no knowledge of her alleged marriage to Dalrymple. It was a very public, bitter and dirty business as the entire proceedings were published and widely distributed in Scotland.[178]

The matter dragged on for over a year. Dalrymple claimed that Mary and her *advisor* (Robert), had only started up her counterclaim to deflect his original suit for defamation of character. This was self evident, he claimed, in that fact that she was absent from diets and had repeatedly withheld details of the supposed marriage to the Commissioners appointed to investigate her claims in Ireland and Gibraltar. He also noted that she was now pregnant by her protector and advisor.

In the interim Robert found the time to write a potted history of his family's connections to the Glencairns entitled: *Genealogy of the Earl of Glencairn and the family of Cunningham* (1740) which he addressed to his cousin Alexander Cunningham of Craigends who owned the Grandvale Estate in Westmoreland, Jamaica. This rambling epistle was never published.[179]

Robert died in Edinburgh in 13 November 1743 by which time Mary had dramatically re-written her personal history. She was no longer the abandoned wife of Captain Dalrymple but, by recent *hidden marriage*, the spouse of the deceased Robert Cunyngham. The result of this short but happy union was their legitimate infant daughter - Susannah.

---

178   NAS CS 271/66626.
179   NAS GD 393/91/5.

Robert Cunyngham's Will

To the astonishment of Daniel and his grieving family, he was informed that his father had re-married and had left a new will, written while he was *standing on the threshold of a new world* in 27 October 1743. One in which Daniel and his family inherited only the family's two sugar plantations and property in St. Kitts. The bulk of the family fortune - the three country estates in Ayrshire - were now left to his step mother's infant girl. This poured oil on the fire of this scandalous affair, rekindling legal battles that lasted twelve years.

Mary made the first move while Daniel was still in St. Kitts. She emptied the Ayrshire houses of their contents *so that they should not be embezzled.* She then petitioned the courts with 'A Bill of Advocation' to have her husband's last will proved. This would transfer all his Scottish property to her as the guardian of his rightful heir and inheritor - Susannah.

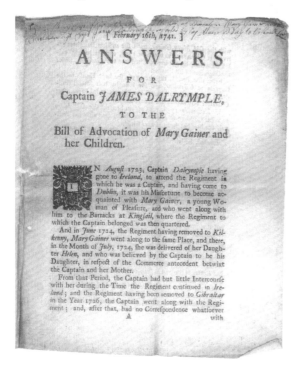

Answers to Mary Gainer's Bill of Advocation

To block her progress, Daniel's eldest sister Elizabeth, living in Dreghorn, immediately started legal proceedings in the Commissary Court in Edinburgh to expose Gainer as a fraud and cheat. This manipulative house keeper, they claimed, had taken advantage of her senile old father and palmed off the child of another as his. The papers from the previous court cases including the statements of Captain Dalrymple were presented as evidence of her duplicity. But Elizabeth was no match for Mary and, without evidence of her previous marriage or Robert's senility, the will was proved.[180]

That was not the end of the matter. In 1745 Mary pushed, as Susannah's guardian, to have a clause in the will activated. This was for the revenue from the St. Kitts plantations (Daniel's inheritance) to pay for any outstanding debts on the Ayrshire estates. As Robert had been in the process of buying a new property known as the 'Holms of Dundonald' at the time of his death, she claimed that Daniel had to pay to complete the purchase (£1008) - which would then be handed it over to her. Daniel came in person to London to contest this interpretation of his father's will through the Court of Chancery. Much to his chagrin, his absence from a crucial hearing in July 1750 clinched the case in favour of his determined step mother.[181] Daniel resurrected the action in the Court of Session of Scotland in January 1758, hoping that Scots Law would take a different view. This was to no avail as their Lordships sitting in Edinburgh upheld the English court's right to hear the case.[182]

The Legacy

By then the formidable Mary Gainer had already shrugged off the scandal of her past life and taken on the full trappings of the landed 'dowager' Cunyngham in Scottish society. Her primary focus was the social promotion her daughter. In this aim she succeeded when Susannah married James

---

180   Mary was highly dismissive of her: *Elizabeth Cunyngham, his daughter, was a disobedient child and married [her cousin a minister in Dreghorn] to his dissatisfaction of both him and her relations who never countermanded her – [Robert] gave [Elizabeth] a legacy of £25 per annum.* January 1744: NAS CS.271/49002. While in St. Kitts, Robert had asked Colonel McDowall of Castlesemple to arrange for her children's education.

181   This case – Conyngham v Conyngham - was heard under English Law (as St. Kitts came under this system) by Lord Chancellor Hardwicke sitting in the Court of Chancery.

182   NAS CS 223/9/2/29.

Dalrymple of Nunraw, the seventh son of Sir Hew Dalrymple of North Berwick in February 1759. Unfortunately, Susannah died in February 1761, leaving two sons who did not live to see their maturity.[183]

Daniel and his wife, with their four children – Elizabeth Philadelphia, Robert, Anthony and Henrietta – did not return to St. Kitts after the last court case. Instead they settled in Ludlow, Shropshire. As absentee plantation owners, their prime asset was left in the hands of managers. Consequently, their upkeep and output suffered at a time when sugar prices were stagnant. As revenue they received slumped so the mortgage on their properties soared to £8,000.[184] Towards the end of the 1750s, during the Seven Years War, Daniel sold off his smaller holdings on

St.Kitts , retaining only the Cayon Plantation, to reduce his exposure.[185] Tragedy struck in 1771 when his eldest son Robert, destined to take up the management of the plantation, died on the island of Monserrat. Daniel died six years later in Curzon Street, Mayfair. Thereafter, his widow Elizabeth returned to her roots, spending the remainder of her life on their Cayon plantation.[186]

Locket portrait with braid hair surround of Robert Cunyngham, son of Daniel. Courtesy of the Faillie Family

---

183   Marriage record in the Edinburgh Parish Register 25 February 1759. Sir Hew was the third son of the celebrated jurist James Dalrymple of Stair, see: Sir James Balfour, *The Scots Peerage* (Edinburgh, 1911) p.141.

184   As early as 1750 Daniel had raised a mortgaged of £14,880 with Robert Calhoun on his c.168 acre Spring Estate in St Mary's that he had just bought from Clement Crooke, Doctor of Physic; National Archives Kew, PROB11/1036 St Kitts Common Records, Index book X, no.1.

185   Losses to French privateers operating in the waters around the Leeward Islands during the early phase of the war threatened to cut off St.Kitts from its provisions. As Robert Colhoun wrote to William McDowall in the summer of 1757; *as all the vessels from the Clyde with herrings are now gone Gods knows what will become of our poor slaves*. He added that he had *settled with Daniel Cunyngham*: NAS GD 237/12/47.

186   She died on the Cayon estate some time after 1777.

Daniel's heir, his second son Anthony, seems to have been more interested in pursuing his claim to the Earl of Glencairn title than running a plantation. And so he signed it over to his only daughter Henrietta and her Belgian husband Stanislas Remi Faille.

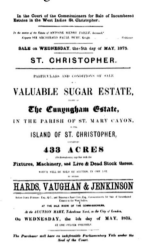

Sale of Cunynghame Plantation, St. Kitts poster (left). Present day remains of the Cayon plantation St. Kitts. Courtesy of the Faille Family (right).

The Cayon plantation (then known as 'Cunynghams') was eventually sold in 1875 ending the family connection with St. Kitts. Little now remains of Robert's handiwork. With end of sugar cropping on the island in the 1950s, his windmill and boiling house have fallen into ruins while the main house was burned to the ground – all within living memory.[187]

---

187   I am indebted to David K. Faille, a descendent of Henrietta Cunyngham, for access to his notes on his research into his family history.

Conclusion

What if Burns had gone to Jamaica?

The 'What if Burns had gone?' scenario can be transposed to those young Scots of conscience who did go out to the West Indies in similar circumstances but returned to fight the great evil of slavery: Zachary Macaulay of Inverary, James Ramsay of Fraserburgh and William Dickson of Moffat.[188] These men manned the intellectual and organisational engine house driving the 'The Society for the Abolition of the Slave Trade'. This movement was founded in London by Thomas Clarkson in 1787, the year after Burns' flirtation with Jamaica.[189]

Macaulay's experience is, arguably, the closest 'fit' to what might have happened had Burns been confronted by the horrors of slavery first hand. Macaulay made few comments during his time on a Jamaican sugar estate. One comment was to admit that, on arrival, he was determined to get over *his squeamishness* and do what was expected of him to drive the slaves at their work in the cane fields. This may be put down to his youth as he was only sixteen years old when he signed indentures as a bookkeeper and

---

188   Dickson was secretary to the Governor of Barbados for thirteen years before he turned objector and returned to London (1786) and offered his services to Clarkson. His herculean efforts during the great campaign of 1792 ensured that one third of all petitions sent to parliament were from north of the border. For a comprehensive review of these men and the Abolitionist movement in Scotland. See: Iain Whyte, *Scotland and the Abolition of Black Slavery* (Edinburgh, 2006).

189   Thomas Clarkson's moral crusade was based on a single objective - cutting off the supply of enslaved Africans to the West Indies. His belief was that, with the trade stopped, the horrific institution of plantation slavery itself would quickly become economically unviable and be replaced by a free labour 'waged' system. He underestimated the tenacity of the 'planter lobby' that fought an effective rearguard action to save their 'property' which perpetuated slavery within the British Empire for another thirty years after the transatlantic slaving ban (1807).

sailed for the plantations (1784).[190]

Zachary Macaulay 1768-1895

By the time he left Jamaica, five years later, he was a 'seasoned' man who could only look back on his time on a slave plantation as: *a period of my life of which I scarce like to speak or think. It was a period of the most degrading servitude to the worst of masters.* Thereafter, as editor of the *Anti-Slavery Reporter*, he dedicated his life to crusading for its abolition.[191]

It is to be hoped that, had Burns gone through such a life changing experience, he would have reacted in a similar way and deployed his observational powers and pen to hasten the end of the suffering of hundreds of thousands of slaves. As it was, he stayed in Scotland and so was largely untouched by the blight on humanity of *half starv'd slaves in warmer skies* thousands of miles away.[192] Indeed, very little seems to have impinged on his consciousness, even though the Abolitionists were highly active in Ayrshire. Two were particularly well known to him: the Rev. John Russell and Rev. William Dalrymple. The hell fire preacher Russell appears as 'black Russell' in *The Holy Fair*, as 'wordy Russell' in *The Twa Herds* and 'Rumble John' in *The Kirks Alarm*. Russell was one

---

190   Modern commentators who suggest that a bookkeeper's role was sufficiently removed from that of the overseer to save Burns from the bloody business of 'driving' slaves in the field are deluding themselves.

191   Zachary Macaulay, who became the first governor of the 'free' colony of Sierra Leone, is the subject of Iain Whyte's *Zachary Macaulay 1768-1838; The Steadfast Scot in the British Anti-Slavery Movement*, Liverpool Studies in International Slavery, 5 (2011). I am grateful to him for his comments.

192   Postscript to *The Author's Earnest Cry and Prayer*.

of the 'auld lichts' who enthusiastically hosted Dickson on his tour of Ayrshire and delivered the financial support of the Irvine Presbytery for the petition campaign. Dalrymple, who had baptised Burns (1759), was described in *The Twa Herds* as 'lang our fae' with the 'auld lichts'. As the one time Moderator of the General Assembly his liberal leanings earned him the title 'D'rymple mild' in *The Kirk's Alarm*. Initially a supporter of the abolitionist cause, he became less than lukewarm after receiving a letter from the West Indies.[193]

The possible exception to Burns' detachment from the slavery issue is the much quoted - *Slave's Lament*. This work was first published in James Johnson's *Scots Musical Museum* in 1792 - the year of the great Abolitionist petition campaign spearheaded by William Dickson in Scotland. But it must be said that the later assertion that Burns was the lyrist is highly

Send Back the Money poster 1846 (left). Frederick Douglass 1818-1895 (right).

---

193   Iain Whyte, *Scotland and the Abolition of the Slave Trade* (Edinburgh, 2006), pp. 77-8.

suspect. [194] Literary critics of the *Lament* are, however, unified in the opinion that, if it was indeed from his pen, it is of a mediocre standard, far removed from the piercing social comment on injustice of which Burns was so capable of at the peak of his powers.

What is without question is that Burns' poems proclaiming the universal 'Brotherhood of Man' motivated future generations of social reformers - notably, the Emancipationists locked in the great struggle to end black slavery in the southern states of America. This goal was only achieved after a bloody civil war in 1865. Twenty years earlier, Frederick Douglass, the great black American champion and present day national icon, took time out from his two year 'Send Back the Money' Scottish campaign to make the pilgrimage to Burns' birthplace in Alloway.[195] In April 1846 he toured the monuments and sights: *I have felt more interest in visiting this place than any other in Scotland, for, as you are aware (painfully, perhaps) I am an enthusiastic admirer of Robert Burns.* He was particularly moved by Highland Mary's bible and lock of her hair, and with his meeting with the eighty-year old 'Mrs Begg' (Burns' youngest sister, Isabella) and two of her daughters. He wrote to a friend in America: *Took my leave - bade farewell. I saw in them so much of what I love in everybody else ... I have ever esteemed Robert Burns, a true soul, but never could I have had the high esteem of the man or his genius. Which I now entertain.*[196]

---

194   There is a school of thought, to which the author subscribes, that the *Lament* is based on an older piece of unknown origin. This is underlined by the fact that it refers to slaving from Senegal to Virginia when the Senegal coast was not a collection point favoured by British slavers, and Virginia had not been part of the British slave trade circuit since 1775.

195   He spoke to packed audiences on two nights in March at the Cathcart Street Church on the issue of the Free Church of Scotland's acceptance of money from slaveholding presbyteries in southern states of America. Douglass later states that he attended a Burns Night in Rochester New York the following year where he paid his dues to the poet who gave him the inspirational insight that – *A man's a man for a' that.*

196   This letter was later published as: 'A Fugitive Slave Visiting the Birth-Place of Robert Burns' *New York Weekly Tribune* 18 July 1846. He met Isabella at her home at the Bridge House in Alloway.

Isabella Burns (Mrs John Begs) 1771-1858

Having stood on the banks of the River Doon, close by the Rozelle and Belleisle estates of the Hamiltons, Douglass astutely concluded: *Burns lived in the midst of a bigoted and besotted clergy – a pious, but corrupt generation – a proud, ambitious and contemptuous aristocracy.* Douglass' eloquent verdict, that of a self-educated fugitive black slave with a price on his head, serves to answer the angst question mark over Burns' Jamaican plantation episode: *Spurning all restraints, he sought a path for his feet, and, like all bold pioneers, he made crooked paths. We may lament it, we may weep over it, but in the language of another, we shall lament and weep with him … He was a brilliant genius, and like all of his class, did much good and evil. Let us take the good and leave the evil, let us adopt his virtues and avoid his vices – let us pursue his wisdom but shun his folly.*

Appendix A

Letters on the impact of the formation of Clarkson's 'Society for the Abolition of the Slave Trade 1789'

Extract from letter from Archibald Cameron at the Rozelle plantation to Sir Adam Fergusson dated 17 September 1789

…The propositions in Parliament relative to the slave trade no doubt made a considerable noise in the island, and caused some alarm and some people were rather apprehensive it might create some tumult amongst the slaves, but I believe few or none ever thought the British Parliament could mean to emancipate the present set of slaves in the islands. We supposed and still hope that this business will end in the mode that you mention. The late laws pass'd here for the government of slaves are perfectly adequate to make them as happy as it is possible for people in their present state of civilisation to be, consistent with the safety of the white inhabitants and with any advantage to their owners, and tho' perhaps it will not be believed by an English mob or some high flown patriots I will venture to say the slaves in this island live happier than the common people of most if not of any country in Europe

… I am perfectly of your opinion that the utmost endeavour ought to be made to raise as many children upon the estate as possible. As you justly observe the vast difference of the sexes is much against this wish. With permission I will give you my humble opinion from whence this difference proceeds and why people run so much upon males in preference to females. The return of crops of estates are supposed to bear a proportion to the number of negroes. Now males do a deal more labour than females, even without making any deduction of the time they are breeding and nursing their children, so that an estate that has half males and the other females will by no means

be upon a footing in point of strength with one that has two thirds males and only one third females. The doctors' informations relative to the bad practices amongst the negroe women are certainly just. It shall be my study to counteract their many evil habits as much as possible[197]. I have fitted up a room near the dwelling house purposely for lying-in women. When ever a wench is brought to bed she can be there attended by the surgeon that attends the estate ....

In a later letter (May 1792) Cameron reported to Sir Adam:

Last month I purchased ten young women for the estate, 7 at £83 and 3 at £81; £824. The price is great, but I am informed the next sales will be even higher yet as it is the general opinion the trade will soon be abolished. I mean, if I can get a good choice, to buy ten more ...

NRAS 3572/3/6

On the reaction to the ending of slavery in the British West Indies and the introduction of the 'apprenticeship system' (whereby former slaves were bound to their master for a further six years 'apprenticeship' though their children under six were immediately freed).

Extract of copy letter from overseer Gray Rutherford at Rozelle to Zachary Kennedy and forwarded to Sir James Fergusson of Kilkerran dated 14 August 1834

But as you and the proprietors must naturally be under great anxiety to hear how things have gone forward with us since slavery ceased and the apprenticeship commenced this I hope will be acceptable although short as it contains no alarming report.

---

197   He was referring to the practice of 'swathing' the new born baby tightly with unclean cloth while the cut of the umbilical cord from the navel is still open. Consequently, tetanus was principal killer of infants.

I have read the new law to the people here some time ago and then explained in a language suited to their comprehension with which they seemed all quite satisfied and after enjoying their three day holidays commencing the 1ˢᵗ August they returned to work on the 4ᵗʰ without a murmur or sulky look and have since continued steady and attentive to their duties during the legal hours of work viz. forty eight and a half hours per week. On several estates in the neighbourhood a good deal of passive resistance to the Law was observable for some days and the Stipendiary Magistrates have met with some clamour and disrespect on their first visits to explain the Law but by a little firmness on their part, and by making a few examples we are now all going on smoothly in the district.

The gentleman whose duty it is to visit in a magisterial capacity, mentions Rozelle with two other properties where he was listened to with exemplary attention and respect. On the North side of the island, particularly in the parish of St Ann's, the negroes on many estates refused to turn out to work, saying the King had made them free, that Lord Mulgrove had told them so and they would not work. The Marquis of Sligo has, however, deal [this] with admirable promptitude. The militia were called out – the steamer was sent round with troops and it is rumoured that these vigorous measures have already had the effect of bringing the Malcontents pretty generally to a sense of their duty. I have no doubt but after a little while all classes and colours will become reconciled in some degree to the changed system. But I fear the diminution of Labour and consequently of crop will be serious felt by all proprietors, more particularly by those who possess small and laborious sugar estates, for they cannot be long maintained I fear. In coffee properties there never been a necessity for night work, and therefore, the change will be less felt. To the Rozelle people I have proposed they work five full days of nine hours each in every week in place of four and a half days out of crop season, and when sugar is being manufactured that they shall keep the mill going from 4 am till 8 pm. In consideration for which they shall continue to receive all the usual allowances of clothing, herrings & all and their children under six years of age, now free, shall be cared for as heretofore. To these terms they have not yet assented but at any rate the bargain must be approved of by the Special Magistrates to be binding on their part, and see that is done. I must defer sending the list of supplies for 1835 – it is ready however. The weather is favourable and the people generally healthy and our [animal] stock are likewise thriving.

Signed

Gray Rutherford, Rozelle.

To which Kennedy added his cover note to Sir James:
I may add that the safest course is to leave Mr Rutherford and the apprentices [former slaves] to settle their own terms. He is sensible and experienced and we are distant and inexperienced.

NRAS 3572/3/39

Appendix B

Burns' neighbours and their slave compensation claims, 1835-6

Many of the occupants of grand houses that stand in and around the parish of Alloway made compensation claims in 1835-6 to the Treasury for the lost of their 'property' following the abolition of slavery in the British Empire. These have recently been catalogued by University College London's *Legacies of the British Slave-ownership* projects.[198]

The combined compensation claims for the Jamaican plantations 'Pemberton Valley' (with its affiliated 'Boscabelle Pen') in St Mary's Parish and 'Rozelle' in the parish of St Thomas-in-the-East alone amounted to £9,237. This is somewhere in excess of three quarters of a million pounds in today's monetary values. As has previously been mentioned, both these large plantations had originally been acquired by Robert Hamilton from

---

198   In 1833 the British government agreed to pay out £20 million in compensation to slave owners for the loss of their 'property' - the men and women who were enslaved. Each owner was listed in a Parliamentary Paper published in 1837-1838 now held in the National Archives at Kew which form the basis of the University College London project - *Legacies of British Slave-ownership*. This project has focused on beneficiaries who were living in Britain at the time of Emancipation or came to Britain thereafter. These absentees amounted to about 2,500-3,000 of the total number of about 29,000 beneficiaries. They received about 40% of the money. One particularly interesting dimension of this is that Scots played a disproportionately important role. Research so far suggests that claimants living in Scotland accounted for at least 15% of absentee owners at a point when the Scottish population was less than 10% of the UK population as a whole. One of the largest single groups receiving compensation were Glasgow & West Coast merchants who seem to have taken about 10% of all compensation paid to British merchants. The database is available online: www.ucl. ac.uk/lbs/research/

Ayr in 1734, upon his extremely advantageous marriage to Jean Mitchell - a Jamaican planter's widow. One hundred years later the ownership of these plantations had devolved to five of the most prominent landed gentry families of South Ayrshire who were all closely linked by marriage. Back in the 1760s Robert had sold his Rozelle sugar plantation soon after retiring back home to Ayrshire from Jamaica. So it was the new owners – the Hunter Blairs of Blairquhan and the Fergussons of Kilkerran – who benefitted from the payout on the Rozelle slaves in 1835.[199]

Robert Hamilton had, however, retained the Pemberton Valley plantation, the ownership of which was split evenly with his brother John's widow - Margaret Montgomerie. So it was passed on after their deaths to their respective heirs. At the time of the compensation payments, Margaret's heirs were the 'Hamiltons of Sundrum Castle' and the 'Hamiltons of Pinmore & Belleisle'. Robert's share had devolved to the heirs of his youngest daughter Eleanora (as his last surviving daughter) who had married Hugh Montgomerie of Coilsfields - latterly 12th Earl of Eglinton. By 1835 both Eleanora and Hugh were dead, as were their three sons, leaving their two surviving daughters as the claimants.

The Pemberton Valley & Boscabelle Pen claims

Claim No. 267 was lodged for the loss of 265 slaves on the Pemberton Valley estate valued at £4580-8/3d for compensation. A further claim No. 269 was lodged for the 42 slaves on the associated Boscabelle Pen which increased the overall award by a further £865-10/3d. There were four claimants. The first named was John Hamilton of Sundrum (III) who had married Christine Dundas of Dundas. The second was Lady Jane Montgomerie, eldest daughter of Eleanora, Countess of Eglinton. The third was Lady Lilias Oswald (nee Montgomerie) second daughter of Eleanora. At the time of the claim she had recently married the widower - Richard Alexander Oswald of Auchencruive and Scotstoun. He was the

---

199   Sir Adam Fergusson served as Rector of Glasgow University and was MP for Ayrshire three times and once for Edinburgh.

heir to the combined fortunes of his great uncle and his father - the liberal MP for Ayrshire.

A further claim (No. 269) was submitted by Thomas Bargany Hamilton - the sixth son of 'Sundrum John' III - for ten slaves on the Pemberton Valley estate. This claim was mostly likely on the private stock accumulated by him whilst he was the resident plantation manager.

The Rozelle claim

There was a single claim (No. 510) for the 198 enslaved on the Rozelle plantation. The award was £3591-8/8d which was split between the current owners - Sir James Fergusson of Kilkerran and Sir David Hunter Blair of Blairquhan.[200] Sir James Fergusson was born in 1765, the eldest son of Sir Adam (the 3rd baronet) who had himself acquired his half of the plantation in 1782 in lieu of debts owed by his brother.[201]

Sir James Hunter Blair, Lord Provost of Edinburgh with city plans in his hand by John Kay

The father of David - Sir James Hunter Blair - was a keen supporter of Burns, cordially receiving him on his arrival in Edinburgh. Indeed, Burns penned an elegy to his patron 'the lamp of day, with ill-presaging glare' on his death in 1787. Sir James was noted as one of the great Lord Provosts of Edinburgh - pushing through the second phase of the New Town and acting as the driving force behind the building of South

---

200   David succeeded to the baronetcy aged 22 when his elder brother died in 1800.

201   James' grandson (also James) went on to become Governor of Southern Australia, New Zealand and Bombay in succession; he was MP for Ayrshire and held numerous government posts before he was killed in the 1907 Jamaican earthquake.

Bridge over the Cowgate, the rebuilding of the Old College in the Old Town, and the building of Bridewell Prison on Calton Hill. He made most of his fortune as a banker with Sir William Forbes and was MP for Edinburgh. Sir David eventually sold his share of the Rozelle plantation in 1848 to Sir Charles Dalrymple-Fergusson who had succeeded to the Kilkerran baronetcy ten years earlier.

As for the monies received, it would appear that much of it was spent on improvements of their Ayrshire estates. It is known that new wings were added to Rozelle mansion in Alloway in 1837, when acquired by Archibald Hamilton of Carcluie (Lilias Montgomerie's grandson and husband of claimant Lady Jane) from his nephew the 13th Earl of Eglinton. Around the same time improvements to Blairquhan Castle (rebuilt 1822-4) were ongoing.

The North Ayrshire claims

The compensation paid (claim No. 333) for the slaves liberated on Cayon estate ('Cunynghames') in the parish of St Mary on St. Kitts was heavily encumbered with large debts and obligations and so it was the creditors who were awarded the £2555 compensation paid out on its 161 slaves.

The root problem lay with the bequeathments in Daniel's will (1761). He left the St. Kitts estate to his surviving son Anthony I, but encumbered its revenue with costly legacies (£2000) to support each of Anthony's two sisters – Elizabeth Philadelphia (who had married Charles Pearce Hall) and Henrietta (who had married John Knight). With Daniel's widow residing in Cayon after his death, their daughters were to receive their legacies only during their life times. Thereafter, the legacies were to be paid to their living offspring. By 1835 there were three 'Miss Halls' awaiting nineteen years unpaid interest since their mother's death (1815) plus their legacy – amounting to £6,000 all in all. This left nothing for the owners of the plantation - Anthony's own son and daughter – Anthony II and Henrietta II (Madame Remi Faille) both described as 'of Lille'.

Anthony II also was unsuccessful in his claim (No. 296) for compensation (£1242-4/5d) for the 76 slaves on the 'Spring Plantation' close by Cayon which his grandfather Daniel had purchased sometime around 1750. The reason being that it had been acquired in lieu of debts to the successful claimant – Charles Adamson – just before the Slavery Compensation Act was passed.

As for the St Kitts estates of Robert Cunyngham's business partners – the McDowalls of Castlesemple and Millikens of Milliken Park, Renfrewshire. McDowalls' Canada Hills estate had been sold thirty years earlier in the scramble to avoid bankruptcy following the collapse of the great West Indian trading house of Alexander Houstoun & Co of Glasgow. The Millikens, however, managed to retain their Monkey Hill estate (then known as 'Millikens') behind Basseterre which allowed Sir Milliken Napier to make a successful claim (No. 226) for his 161 slaves totalling £2555-1/2d.

The descendent of Robert Cunyngham's cousins – William Cunninghame of Craigends – was still in control of the Grandvale estate in Jamaica in 1835. Along with his trustees – Alexander Pearson, James Stirling and William Houstoun – he received compensation amounting to £3,278-5/6 for a claim (no.453) for 185 slaves on the estate.

In all cases the freed slaves received nothing.

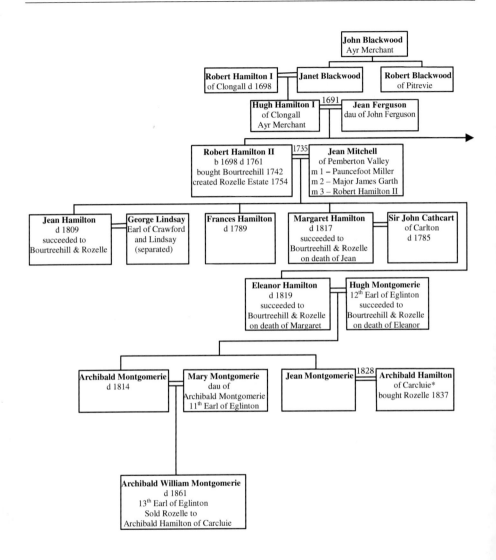

Appendix C

The HAMILTON'S of BOURTREEHILL, ROZELLE, SUNDRUM, PINMORE and BELLEISLE until c.1850

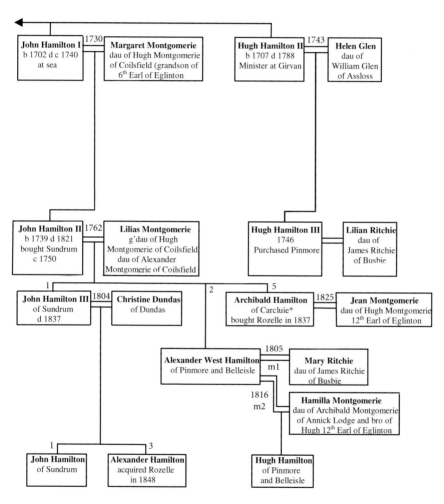

Appendix D

The FERGUSSON'S of KILKERRAN

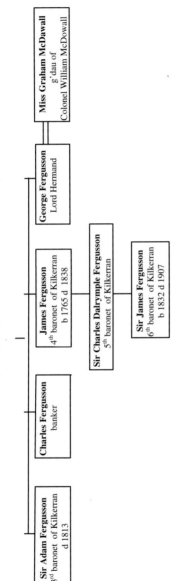

The HUNTER BLAIR'S of BLAIRQUHAN

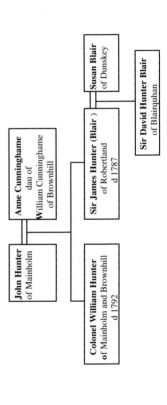

Appendix E

The OSWALD'S of AUCHENCRUIVE until c.1750

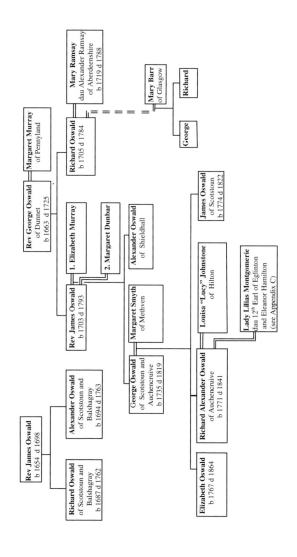

Appendix F

The CUNYNGHAM'S of BAIDLAND until c.1800

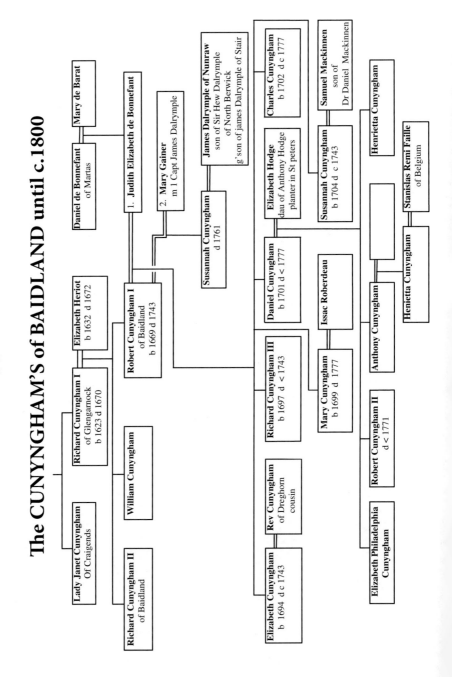

Bibliography

Primary Sources

Ayrshire Archives

AA/ DC 13 & 17 Hamilton papers
AA/ DC 191 Hunter Blair papers

National Archives Kew

PROB11/1036 St Kitts Common Records

National Archives of Scotland

NAS GD 3/3 Pemberton Valley Plantation accounts
NAS GD 142/2 Hugh Hamilton papers
NAS GD 205/53 Tullideph papers
NAS GD 213/54 Richard Oswald correspondence
NAS GD 237/12 Colhoun papers
NAS GD 393/91 Alexander Boyd letters
NAS CS 96/3096-3106 Robert Cunynghame ledgers
NAS CS 271/49002 Cunynghame v Gainer
NAS CS 271/66626 Gainer v Dalrymple
NAS RH 15/54 Burd papers

National Register of Archives Scotland

NRAS 3572 Fergusson Papers

National Library of Scotland

NLS Acc.7285 Clark letters
NLS Ms 586 Watson Collection

Primary Printed

Ayr Advertiser
Barnard, John, *A present to the Apprentice or a Sure Guide to Wealth and Esteem* (London, 1807)
Caribbeana Vols. I –V
Donan, Elizabeth, *Documents Illustrative of the History of the Slave Trade*, Vol. IV, (Washington, 1935)
Edinburgh Evening Courant
Garden, Alexander, *Dr Alexander Garden of Charles Town* (Chapel Hill, 1969)
Jamaica Almanack (1811)
Glasgow Mercury
McQuhae, William, *Difficulties which Attend the Practice of Religion No Just Argument Against It,*
New York Weekly Tribune
Schaw, Janet, *Journal of a Lady of Quality*, edited by Evangeline Walker Andrews (Nebraska, 2005)
Smith, Thomas, *Narrative of an unfortunate voyage to the coast of Africa* (Arbroath, 1813)
Ramsay, James, *Essays on Slavery* (1784).
Robinson, Samuel, *The Experiences of a Boy Sailor aboard a slave ship* (Hamilton, 1867)
Register of the Privy Council of Scotland (3 series, Vol. XIV)
The Scots Peerage (Edinburgh, 1911)

Books & Articles

Anon, *Marly; or, A Planter's Life in Jamaica*, edited by Karina Williamson (Oxford, 2005)
Barclay, Tom & Eric J. Graham, 'The Covenanters Colony in Carolina', *History Scotland* Vol.4, No.4 (Ayr, 2004)
Barclay, Tom & Eric J. Graham, *The Early Transatlantic Trade of Ayr (1640-1730)*, Ayrshire Archaeological and Natural History Society monograph

30 (Ayr, 2005)

Brady, Frank, 'So Fast To Ruin'. *AANHS* Vol. 11, No.2

Carruthers, Gerald and others, 'Burns & Slavery', *Fickle Man,* (Dingwall, 2009)

Devine, T.M., 'Transport Problems of Glasgow West India merchants during the American War of Independence, 1775-83' *Transport History* Vol. IV, *(1971)*

Graham, Eric J., 'Abolitionists and apologists: Scotland's Slave Trade Stories', *Discover NLS,* Issue 6 (2007)

Graham, Eric J., *A Maritime History of Scotland 1765-1790* (East Linton, 2002)

Graham, Eric J., 'Sugar Plantocrats – the Cunynghams of Glengarnock and Cayon St.Kitts' *History Scotland,* Vol. 7 No.8 (2007)

Graham, Eric J., 'The Slaving Voyage of the *Hannover* of Port Glasgow 1719-20' *History Scotland,* Vol. 3, No.5 (2003),

Graham, Eric J., *Seawolves: Pirates & the Scots* (Edinburgh, 2005)

Graham, Eric J., 'Black People in Scotland during the Slavery Era', *Scottish Local History,* issue 71 (2007)

Hancock, David, *Citizens of the World* (Cambridge, 1995)

Limon, Thomas, 'The Roup of the Lands of Alloway', *Ayrshire in the Time of Burns,* AANHS (1959)

Paterson, George, *History of the County of Ayr,* Vol. II (Edinburgh, 1852)

Robertson, George, *A Genealogical Account of the Principal Families in Ayrshire more particularly in Cunninghame,* Vol. I (Edinburgh, 1823)

Shaw, James, *Ayrshire 1745 – 1970, A Social and Industrial History* (Edinburgh, 1953)

Sheridan, Richard, *Sugar and Slavery: an economic history of the British West Indies* (Barbados, 1974)

Whyte, Iain, *Scotland and the Abolition of the Slave Trade* (Edinburgh, 2006)

Whyte, Iain, *Zachary Macaulay 1768-1838; The Steadfast Scot in the British Anti-Slavery Movement,* Liverpool Studies in International Slavery, No. 5 (2011).

Websites

Ayrshire Archives, 'Black History Month' website: http://www.
ayrshirearchives.org.uk/exhibition/blackhist/index.htm
Learning & Teaching Scotland, 'Scotland & Abolition of the Slave Trade'
http://www.ltscotland.org.uk/abolition/index.asp
University College London, *Legacies of British Slave ownership* database:
http://www.ucl.ac.uk/lbs/search

Index